The DREAM BEGINS

HOW HAWAI'I SHAPED BARACK OBAMA

To
Linda + Carlos
Feb 14, 2009

THE DREAM BEGINS

HOW HAWAI'I SHAPED BARACK OBAMA

STU GLAUBERMAN AND JERRY BURRIS

WATERMARK
PUBLISHING

ISBN 978-0-9815086-8-9

Library of Congress Control Number: 2008933771

Design and production
Marisa Oshiro

Cover Design
Nelson Marehalau

Cover photography courtesy of Maya Soetoro-Ng and Obama for America

Front cover quote by Michelle Obama reprinted with permission of David Mendell from *Obama: From Promise to Power* (HarperCollins Books, 2007)

Watermark Publishing
1088 Bishop St., Suite 310
Honolulu, Hawai'i 96813
Telephone 1-808-587-7766
Toll-free 1-866-900-BOOK
sales@bookshawaii.net
www.bookshawaii.net

Printed in the United States

Contents

FOREWORD
BY HAWAI'I CONGRESSMAN NEIL ABERCROMBIE

On December 28, 2003, at Kualoa Ranch on the Hawaiian Island of O'ahu, overlooking a vast stretch of the western Pacific Ocean, Maya Soetoro married Konrad Ng. The evening was presided over by Maya's brother, Illinois State Senator Barack Obama. After the ceremony, he stepped forward to address assembled friends including myself and my wife, Nancie Caraway. His voice was cool and soothing, his manner loose and inviting, Island-style. So different, I thought, from his father's commanding baritone and intense presence.

Barack spoke of family—*'ohana* to the Hawaiians—the coming together of the world in Hawai'i, that day made manifest by the union of his Indonesian-*haole* sister and his new Chinese-Canadian brother-in-law, all within the embrace of the spirit of *aloha*. His remarks centered on how, in Hawai'i, our diversity defines us rather than divides us. He said that was a message the world needed to hear from the rainbow people of Hawai'i. In that diversity was the hope of the world. We were all *'ohana*.

My mind flooded with thoughts of his African father and *haole*—Hawaiian for Caucasian—mother from the Mainland. I had met them at the University of Hawai'i in Honolulu just after Statehood in 1959. Barack's father was determined to be a part of the birth of a free Kenya, just as the civil rights movement his mother had championed was breaking through old boundaries in the United States, not the least of which was statehood for multicultural Hawai'i.

Now here was their son speaking of a vision of hope in a changing world, the concept of community and family living in harmony, within our grasp if we would commit ourselves to it. I heard echoes of his parents' dream of a renewed world in Barack's voice and words as he held the crowd with his vision. Not a speech, not ritual remarks, but a conversation unfolded, almost a series of intimate observations from a friend to an extended family. It was mesmerizing.

I turned to Nancie and said, "He's going to be the President one day." Nancie, later in the evening, teasingly asked Michelle Obama, "He's the real deal, isn't he?" Michelle replied deadpan: "He's the real deal."

The nation saw and heard what we experienced on that wedding day when Barack had another conversation, this time with the people of the United States. In his keynote address to the Democratic National Convention in Boston in 2004, Barack spoke to and about the American *'ohana*. His speech propelled him into the front ranks of Democratic political figures as he contended for a U.S. Senate seat in Illinois.

After his victory that fall Barack, Michelle and their daughters came to Honolulu for their annual Christmas visit to see his family and the high school friends with whom he'd never lost touch. With the defeat of John Kerry, he was fast emerging as the brightest star in the American political firmament. At an event at the Hilton Hawaiian Village in Waikīkī to celebrate his election as Hawai'i 's "third Senator," Barack was visibly moved. It was apparent that the enthusiasm of the crowd that night was the begin ning of a great wave that would roll across the nation.

We know something about waves in Hawai'i. We know that no matter how high, how broad, how powerful, every wave eventually dissipates in the sand. You either ride it when it comes or it rushes over you and inexorably crashes on the shore. Whatever his ambitions or plans, events were overtaking everything. It mattered little that he had just been elected to the U.S. Senate. My wife said simply and directly, "You can't time timing."

We were only two of a swelling multitude of voices expressing the growing sentiment that Barack had to run for president. What began as a campaign was to become a movement.

Taylor Branch, the biographer of Dr. Martin Luther King, in addressing the civil rights struggle, described a movement as "faith in strangers." Barack Obama was not just engaged in an election campaign; millions of us joined with him in a movement—a movement away from fear and callous indifference. We might have been strangers in that we had never met, but we were as one in our belief in the possibility of real democratic change.

On the day of the Iowa caucus that would likely decide whether his campaign was real or only a dream, Barack disappeared from the clamor and glare of the campaign trail. He was playing basketball with friends and former classmates who had flown from Hawai'i to Des Moines to be with him. His *'ohana* was there. They had brought Hawai'i to him.

After campaigning for Barack across the state of Iowa that day,

I joined the rally watching the returns in Des Moines. When the news came, people poured out of the arena shouting "We won! We won!" I knew then that everything was *pono* (correct, proper)—all had been made right.

Aloha,
Neil Abercrombie
U.S. House of Representatives

CHAPTER ONE

"IN NO OTHER COUNTRY ON EARTH"
STEPPING ONTO A WORLD STAGE

Few Americans had heard of Barack Obama when he stepped up to give the keynote speech at the 2004 Democratic National Convention in Boston. The political rookie strode to the podium with youthful vigor. Dressed in a dark suit that fit to perfection, he was a towering figure with an imposing presence. At 42, Obama was a fresh-faced state senator from Illinois running for election to the United States Senate. Though people in Chicago admired the former community organizer and civil rights lawyer, he was not well known beyond his home state. Minutes into his speech, his obvious confidence and infectious optimism commanded the attention of convention delegates and a national TV audience. It was as if a star were being born. Each televised image established that Obama was not your typical American politician.

He couldn't hide it. In fact, he made a point of saying that his appearance in the national spotlight as a "skinny guy with a funny-sounding name" was a particular and unusual honor. As he put it, his father was born and raised in a small village in Kenya and grew up herding goats. His mother was from a small town half a world away in Kansas. They gave him an African name, Barack, because they believed that in America, an out-of-the-ordinary name was no barrier to success. It took him a while to grow into that name, but upon reaching manhood, he proved them right. He stood there, facing a worldwide audience, and acknowledged that he was grateful for the diversity of his heritage. He proclaimed himself a shining example of the American Dream and acknowledged, "In no other country on Earth is my story even possible."

In that Democratic National Convention speech that electrified a nation and put him on the path to the presidency, Barack Obama observed that America's greatness lay in neither its skyscrapers nor its awesome military power. America's strength and genius resided, he said, in the simple premise stated in the Declaration of Independence, that all men are created equal, with the same God-given rights to pursue happiness. He told of his fundamental belief that every American *is* his or her brother's and sister's keeper, and that just like a family member, every citizen is responsible for the success and happiness of all. The core idea that awakened a nation was that in 2004 there was not a black America or a white America, or a Latino or an Asian America. In a call that sounded loud and clear and eventually echoed among the disenfranchised, Obama envisioned a politics of purpose that united people and lifted them above the tunnel vision of partisanship and special interests. In what political analysts quickly labeled a political speech for the ages, Obama cautioned Americans not to let "spin-masters and ad peddlers" poison their thoughts and divide the country. It was a lofty notion for a man who would soon become mired in the muck of one of the longest presidential campaigns in America's history yet still stand tall as a lightning rod for positive change.

Despite his unusual name and his unique background, or perhaps because of them, Obama positioned himself as a bridge-builder, someone who could bring together the nation's diverse races, religions and regions. Here was a man who straddled the races, being half white and half black; and who straddled the regions, having lived on the East Coast and the West Coast, in the Midwest and the Pacific, and in Asia as well. Could this be the man who could help Americans bridge painful, centuries-old, historical racial and regional divisions? That promise of change, plus a few remarkably lucky political breaks, helped Obama win election as the only African-American in the United States Senate in 2005, and only the third black senator in American history. Following his election to the Senate, he published a book about the American Dream. He called it *The Audacity of Hope*. That phrase, borrowed from his Chicago minister, also appeared in his convention speech when he noted that God's greatest gift to America was a belief in things that can't be seen, and that better days are ahead. This God-granted gift was the gift of hope, he said: hope in the face of difficulty and uncertainty. This was the audacity of hope.

How audacious was it to envision a political system blind to color and steadfast in its principles of justice and liberty for all? How audacious was it to suggest that there was a common, non-racial or post-racial set of values that defined the people of our country as Americans? How audacious was it for the youngest U.S. senator to champion a global vision of the 21st century and share it with older, more traditional politicians and expect them to follow his lead? After hearing him speak, after opening their minds, leaders and followers fell in line behind him.

Later, in announcing his candidacy for the Democratic Party's 2008 presidential nomination, Barack Obama boldly challenged the established Democratic hierarchy and its political wisdom. In 1960, many people had dismissed U.S. Senator John Kennedy's chances of becoming president because he was a Catholic and there had never been a Catholic president before him. Half a century later, here was Obama, the Tiger Woods of presidential politics, daring Americans to choose as their next president a man of mixed race who chose emphatically to define himself as an African-American. Despite the distractions of a drawn-out and at times dirty primary campaign, Obama stayed on point with a philosophy of optimism and hope for America's future. His rally cry for change aroused and energized tens of thousands of young people who had only known white Southern-born presidents beholden to legions of special-interest lobbyists. There was something different about Obama, not only in the way he looked but also in the way he thought. There was something in his manner that reached out and drew people in, as if they were being welcomed into a family that would look after one another and care for each other.

Only when the American people got to know Barack Obama as a candidate for president did they learn that the urbane big-city lawyer and Chicago community organizer had been born and raised in Hawai'i. Indeed, Illinois' Senator Obama spent most of his first 18 years anchored to family and friends in Honolulu, where he was known as Barry. Before he was a politician in a well-tailored suit, he was a lanky kid with a trimmed Afro who loved to bodysurf and dreamed of moving to the U.S. Mainland to be an NBA star. It is hard to imagine this highly poised politician as an insecure youth who felt the pain of being left behind by his parents, who sought to define himself racially in an America that seemed split between black and white, while growing up in a community that was rainbow-hued. The nation would eventually come to envision Barack Obama as the first African-American presidential nominee from a major party. But in his birthplace of Honolulu, he would be known as the first Island-born son of Hawai'i who might become president; a perfect example of the proud, mixed-race ideal that Hawai'i had come to honor and reward. And as he rose to fame, his words about unity, hope and caring for one another sounded more and more like the terms of reference that kept Hawai'i on keel as the nation's most intercultural state. No other state could claim to be the Aloha State, an affirmation of the caring and compassion that create and nurture appreciation, understanding and tolerance toward others.

Barack Obama is a man with an amazing life story, quite unlike that of anyone who has ever been nominated for president. It is a story impossible to properly tell without understanding Hawai'i and the times that shaped him and his family.

Just how much Barack Obama owes to the physical and social environment of his first 18 years is something only he knows with certainty. But he has repeatedly said his early childhood and private-school education in Hawai'i, and the people and cultural influences of his home state, have molded the values and worldview he holds today. Longtime educator Siegfried Ramler, who oversaw curriculum development at Punahou, the prep school Obama attended, says you cannot draw a straight line between what Obama did and saw in Hawai'i and what he would do as a world leader. But, says Ramler, the cultural milieu of a youngster's formative years plants millions of seeds that bear fruit in later life. Hawai'i offered a rich multicultural environment under a uniquely evolving racial rainbow.

Although he rightfully and understandably credits the tough streets and rough-and-tumble world of Chicago for his foundation as a politician, Obama says his upbringing in Hawai'i provided the basic values at his very core.

"No place else," he told a Honolulu audience in December 2004, "could have provided me with the environment, the climate, in which I could not only grow but also get a sense of being loved. There is no doubt that the residue of Hawai'i will always stay with me, and that it is part of my core, and that what's best in me, and what's best in my message, is consistent with the tradition of Hawai'i."

During the run-up to the 2008 Hawai'i Democratic caucuses at which a presidential candidate would be chosen, Obama acknowledged that Hawai'i's multiculturalism, in which no ethnic group is dominant, had played a significant role in his development. And in a letter to his half-sister, Maya Soetoro-Ng, who lives in Honolulu, Obama envisioned the uplifting influence Hawai'i would have on his presidential campaign. He wrote: "Hawai'i is a fabulous model for the kind of America I hope this campaign will bring about, a place where different cultures can come together in harmony, and a place that rises above the barriers that divide us."

A talented writer, Obama has described how he felt at home in the Islands, and how he longed to return because Hawai'i was a constant for him. He has written lyrically about Hawai'i, using some of his most poetic phrases to describe the touchstone things he remembered about his first home, even as more and more of his home island of O'ahu became covered with concrete.

"Even now," he wrote in his 1995 memoir, *Dreams from My Father*, "I can retrace the first steps I took as a child and be stunned by the beauty of the Islands. The trembling blue pane of the Pacific. The moss-covered cliffs and the cool rush of Mānoa Falls, with its ginger blossoms and high canopies filled with the sound of invisible birds. The North Shore's thunderous waves, crumbling as if in a slow-motion reel."

And he has said that his worldview and the fundamentals of his values sprang from the experience of living in Hawai'i, where people of different cultures live in what he called "a climate of mutual respect."

That much-envied environment of respect and tolerance, embodied in the shorthand phrase "the Aloha Spirit," was forged and shaped by Hawai'i's status as an island, or more properly a chain of islands that make up the nation's only island state. The Aloha Spirit today derives from the deep spring of Polynesian culture and the overlay of evangelical Christianity, which Hawaiians wholeheartedly embraced and made their own nearly two centuries ago. Three of the core values inherent in this environment are *aloha*, which means love or compassion, *lōkahi*, which means unity, and *'ohana*, which is the Hawaiian word for family, and embraces any relative or a group that can be an extended family of friends, neighbors and co-workers. In a sense, these Hawaiian concepts were at the heart of Obama's political appeal, and they were evidenced in his key themes: the need to look after one another; the need to unify and heal the divisions that keep us apart; and the need to bring every race, religion and region into the American family. There is, without a doubt, an "Island way."

Obama saw a paradox in the fact that his easygoing Hawai'i upbringing pushed him to work in Chicago's South Side, a very different environment. "The irony is that my decision to work in politics, and to pursue such a career in a big Mainland city, in some sense, grows out of my Hawaiian upbringing," he said. That's because Hawai'i instilled in him the idea that with the right attitude, people could live and work together in harmony. Obama's journey from Hawai'i to Chicago, then, was also part of his journey to find himself.

Looking back at his formative years, candidate Obama said: "The essence of Hawai'i has always been that we come from far and wide, that we come from different backgrounds, and different faiths and different last names, and yet we come together as a single *'ohana* because we believe in the fundamental commonality of people."

In June 1963, when Barry was not yet two years old, President Kennedy flew to Honolulu to address a national meeting of mayors on the burning question of how municipalities could help ensure the civil rights of black

Americans. Upon his arrival at the airport, Kennedy delivered remarks highlighting what he envisioned as the ideal mixing of races on the island of O'ahu: "Reaching into the Pacific, yet part of the United States, this island represents all that we are and all that we hope to be," he declared. Forty-five years later, Kennedy's hopeful thought would become part of Obama's own presidential campaign. ೞ

CHAPTER TWO

"A 10-year-old's nightmare"
Starting School in Honolulu

When he arrived home in Hawai'i from Indonesia, he was a chubby, brown-skinned boy with kinky black hair atop a round face with a shy smile. He had traveled from Jakarta to Honolulu on his own, a journey that's twice as long as a flight from New York to California. In the summer of 1971, Barry Obama was 10 years old. Though he'd been born in Hawai'i, his mother had whisked him off to Indonesia when he was six. He attended grades one through four in Jakarta, where classes were taught in the Indonesian language Bahasa Indonesia. His mother used to wake him at 4 a.m. so that she could tutor him in English and typical American subjects for three hours before he left for Indonesian school. Finally she told him that they had gone as far as they could go with correspondence courses. The good news was that Barry would not have to wake up at four anymore. The bad news was that he would have to leave his mother and baby sister and his elementary school friends behind so that he could start fifth grade in Honolulu.

On the way through U.S. Customs, Barry hand-carried a carved wooden mask with a nutty cinnamony smell that exuded its tropical origins. Even before he stepped through the sliding glass doors of International Arrivals, Barry saw his grandparents: the tall, silver-haired man he called Gramps, and the owlish, grandmotherly woman he called Toot. A year earlier, he had come from Jakarta to spend the summer months with Gramps and Toot. It was a summer of going to the beach and eating American ice cream. But on this day of arrival and homecoming, a thought struck Barry like the rock an Indonesian playmate had once thrown at his head. His grandparents were white. Though they had helped raise him in his infancy in the Islands, and he had summered with them, he had never thought of his mother's parents in that way before.

In Southeast Asia, Barry was singled out for being bigger and darker-skinned than his peers. Now he was consigned to living with these white Americans, who seemed like strangers to him. To ease the discomfort of the moment, he pressed the big wooden mask to his face and did a little native dance. Gramps and Toot laughed at his bravado. Outside Customs, his grandparents hugged him and threw a candy *lei* around his shoulders. While flower *lei* were a more traditional greeting, Toot thought her grandson would prefer a store-bought garland of candy and chewing gum held together by a plastic mesh net and spaced apart like blossoms. On the way to his grandparents' apartment, Barry looked out at Honolulu's used-car lots and fast-food restaurants. There weren't yet any McDonalds in Jakarta, and for much of the time he'd lived there, his Indonesian stepfather did not own a car. He had entered a new world, an American world as strange to him as Asia would have been to Hawai'i kids. What made the homecoming even stranger was that Barry's grandparents had moved from the single-family house they had lived in when he'd last visited to a small two-bedroom apartment on the 10th floor of the Punahou Circle Apartments. It was an ordinary-looking apartment building that still stands on South Beretania Street near the heart of Honolulu's commercial district. The nice thing about Gramps' apartment was that it was less than half a mile from the school he would be attending. Toot lives there to this day.

When adults meet for the first time in Hawai'i, they ask, "What school you wen grad?" This is the local pidgin, or mixed-language creole, for "What school did you graduate from?" In many parts of the United States, adults answer this question by naming their college. In Hawai'i, local people invariably answer with the name of their high school. This is because most Hawai'i-born people live on the same island all their lives and remain closely connected to their high school friends. For many Hawai'i residents, the name of a person's high school, or even the nickname of its athletic teams, tells a lot about the person they're meeting for the first time. For starters, it pins down the neighborhood that person grew up in. If someone says McKinley Tigers or Roosevelt Rough Riders, they're from the central business district of Honolulu and grew up among the ethnic groups downtown. If they say Kaiser or Kalani, they're from the suburbs of East Honolulu, which have a different, generally more Caucasian population mix. If they say Punahou, they are at once envied and scorned. The private prep school called Punahou has a well-deserved reputation for academic excellence, athletic championships and physical facilities on a par with national universities. In highly exaggerated local lore, a Punahou education was considered an invitation to the Ivy League and a free pass to enter Hawai'i's elite circles. While it was not required for admission to Punahou, a highly developed superiority complex seemed a byproduct of a Punahou education. For more than 150 years, public high school kids have derided Punahou as a school for rich kids, rich *white* kids. It's the private school's rep, though, not its reality.

Founded in 1841, Punahou School is one of the oldest, largest and wealthiest prep schools west of the Mississippi River. Once known as O'ahu College, the school as a whole is on the National Register of Historic Places. Pronounced "*Poo*-na-ho," the name can be translated as "new spring." For Barry Obama, going to Punahou was certainly a springboard into a new life.

For many students, a Punahou education was indeed a passport to a top college and an entrée into Hawai'i's higher social and business circles. But not every kid at Punahou was born with a silver spoon. Indeed, the majority of these private school pupils were children of bureaucrats, hard-working middle-class families and, yes, the children of public school teachers, who struggled to meet the financial burdens of tuition and fees and other requisites of their children's Punahou lifestyle. Some, like Barry, were fortunate to receive financial aid to make the dream of a prep school education come true. Even so, when it came to living a life of privilege, Barry Obama had to be at the bottom rung of the Punahou student body. He was the son of a single mom, who had no real home of her own and no life savings. He would recall that she struggled to pay the bills and was ashamed to use food stamps to supplement her budget. Yet here he was being schooled alongside the scions of the Islands' wealthiest families, some of whom lived in hillside manors with sparkling swimming pools.

Gramps was excited about his grandson's induction into the Punahou family, as if it promised a higher level of community acceptance for him and Toot, who had lived quiet, unassuming lives in Honolulu for 11 years. As the first day of school neared, Gramps and Barry went over the list of Things to Buy and Things to Do again and again. They knew what to expect from the school grounds, which they had toured the year earlier during the admission process. What Barry didn't know, and had dreaded all summer long, was what it would be like to be among the Punahou students, who were regarded by other Hawai'i kids as a spoiled and snooty breed unto themselves. The worst among them were the few elitists who were inclined to put others down because their clothes didn't match or their teeth needed straightening. What would they think of Barry, the new kid who was not only new but was also half-black, half-white and fresh-off-the-boat from Southeast Asia?

Gramps was one of those people who always left extra time for unexpected eventualities that seldom arise. As a consequence, he always arrived with time to spare. On the first day of school, Gramps and Barry set out early and walked the four blocks up Punahou Street, past the landmark Central

Union Church and the hospital where Barry was born. After crossing Wilder Avenue, they came upon century-old lava-rock walls and Punahou's impressive ornamental iron gates. Insiders viewed those wrought-iron gates as welcoming; outsiders saw them as forbidding. The wide campus drive stretched ahead, bordered by stately palms and perfectly manicured lawns. Forty or more buildings were spread as far as the eye could see over the 76-acre country club-like campus. The oldest building, called Old School Hall, was built in 1851 with the help of students and oxen that carried stone from the mountain slope above the school. The original fresh-water spring that gave the school its name was now encased in lava rock curbstones to create a picturesque lily pond. About five years earlier, the school had covered part of the lily pond fed by *Ka Punahou* (the new spring) with the modernistic Thurston Memorial Chapel, a place of reflection, refuge and worship. Students were required to attend services there at least once a week.

All this was impressive enough, but Barry was more interested in the athletic complex with hard-surface tennis courts, a heated Olympic swimming pool and Olympic track facilities. Hidden from view were a photo lab, a glass-blowing workshop and a jewelry-making studio. Upon seeing the school and the richness of its physical facilities for the first time, Gramps, who had grown up in hard times during the Depression, told Barry: "This isn't a school. This is heaven." Gramps had gone to college briefly on the G.I. Bill immediately after World War II but never earned a degree. Like his father and stepfather, who had achieved their education through scholarships, Barry could not have gone to a school like Punahou without financial aid based on need and the promise of future achievement. To his credit, Gramps had set the wheels in motion for Barry to be admitted to Punahou by prevailing good-naturedly upon his boss, a Punahou graduate, to use his connections as an alumnus to get Barry an interview and a scholarship.

Now, together they walked in the general direction of Diamond Head, visible in the distance, toward the eastern edge of the campus until they finally reached Castle Hall. Though the three-story building looked like a small hotel, it housed only the fifth and sixth grades. Gramps and Barry had started out so early that when they got there, the classroom building was not yet open and only one other kid was there, also a new kid. Gramps made introductions, slapped the two of them on the back, and left Barry to fend for himself on his first day at an American school.

Barry didn't know it, but the new school clothes chosen by Gramps signaled his newness and low place in the socio-economic pecking order.

At Punahou School, families that weren't well off dressed their kids in more expensive school clothes. In a reversal of status symbols, the children of CEOs and stay-at-home moms wore worn-out hand-me-downs from siblings. Rattier clothes indicated greater wealth. That's because the kids who didn't need to dress to impress chose the most comfortable attire for long days at school that involved lots of walking across fields and playing in PE and on the playgrounds. The "in" crowd didn't wear neat Levi's. Their idea of comfort and style was a faded T-shirt and well-worn pants. And they didn't wear buffalo-hide sandals like Barry's.

When Castle Hall finally opened, Barry entered the classroom and sat at a table with four other students assigned to Mrs. Mabel Hefty's homeroom. Seated in Barry's first homeroom class were kids who were ethnically Hawaiian, mixed Hawaiian-Portuguese, mixed Chinese-Caucasian, all-Chinese, all-Caucasian (including an exchange student from Finland) and a kid who was Hawaiian-Tahitian-French.

Mabel Hefty was a short, lively woman who wore distinctively Hawaiian *mu'umu'u*. A native of Brooklyn, New York, who had lived for a time in San Francisco, Mrs. Hefty had left those shores behind for her home in Hawai'i, where she seemed to fit right in. Barry's other fifth-grade teacher was a sports-addicted, part-Hawaiian graduate of Punahou named Pal Eldredge, who was in his first year as a teacher and had been paired with the far more experienced Mabel Hefty. Eldredge believes school officials deliberately placed Barry with Mrs. Hefty because of her interest in Kenya; she had spent a sabbatical there about a year earlier.

As was her ritual on the first day of class, Mrs. Hefty read aloud the name of every child. In Hawai'i, the reading of the class list sometimes sounds like the memorable comedy routine by the late local comedian Rap Reiplinger, a Punahou grad. In Rap's "Japanese Roll Call," one multisyllabic Japanese surname starts where the syllables of the previous one leave off: "Tanemitsu, Mitsuyoshi, Yoshimura, Murakami, Kamikawa, Kawamatsu, Matsutaka, Takahashi, Hashimoto, Motooka, Okafune, Funeshige." Hawai'i kids are used to names like these, but when Mrs. Hefty called out, "Barack Obama," the class erupted in titters over the unusual-sounding name. It would lead him to tell people who stumbled over his name at their first meeting: "Just call me Barry." His African father had done the same thing during his days in Hawai'i.

Though Barry wanted nothing so much as to be ordinary and unsung on that first day, Mrs. Hefty went on to tell the class what she had learned from Gramps. "Boys and girls," she said, "Barack's father came from Kenya", "that beautiful country" where she had taught on sabbatical. When she asked Barry what tribe his father hailed from, he said "Luo." As he remembered it, a sandy-haired *haole* (white) kid started making monkey noises, and the class erupted in laughter. Some of his classmates think the hilarity was based on the fact that "Luo" sounded like "*lua*," the Hawaiian word for toilet. It seemed like forever before Mrs. Hefty moved on to the next student's name, and it didn't get any better after that. After class, a girl with red hair asked if she could touch Barry's hair, and another classmate asked if Barry's father ate people. The best defense was a good offense, so in the weeks to come, Barry made up the story that his father was a great African chief, and that made him a prince.

No matter where Barry looked, there was no one who looked like him. There were about 2,000 kids in kindergarten through grade 12 at Punahou School that year and only a handful were black. In the entire fifth grade, there was only one other black kid, and too bad for Barry, the other student was a girl. When classmates saw Barry talking to the black girl, they taunted him about her being his girlfriend. To show it wasn't so, he shoved her away. It was a socially clumsy and immature act he immediately regretted and one that would require an apology later, when others weren't looking.

Barry was different from the other kids in many ways beyond his buffalo-leather sandals. His father was an African intellectual who chose career advancement over being with his son, and went off to Harvard, leaving a two-year-old boy fatherless. His mother both mollycoddled him and set him loose in a Southeast Asian country, letting him struggle to meet friends with a limited ability in the Indonesian language. When he lived in Jakarta, Barry had stood out from the nut-brown kids in his Catholic and Muslim schools, and now, in this missionary-built prep school in Honolulu, he stood out in a sea of clean-scrubbed Asian-American and white American faces. In Asia, he had spent time flying kites and playing badminton and chess and *futbal*, which Americans called soccer. Hawai'i kids were interested in things Barry knew little or nothing about: baseball, football, skateboards and surfing. They had grown up eating hamburgers and pizza, along with local favorites like *sushi*, *kālua* pig, *lū'au* squid, Portuguese sausage, *kim chee*, *choi sum*, broiled eel and the local limpets called *'opihi*. Even so, he couldn't very well tell his new class-mates that in Jakarta he had eaten dog meat, snake meat and grasshoppers.

Punahou School prides itself on multiculturalism. Its curriculum and its recommended course for student life celebrate foreign language and culture and the world's religious traditions, going beyond the teaching of tolerance to virtually preaching participation in the global community.

After reading the school's admission materials, one would imagine that Punahou students would have welcomed Barry Obama with open arms. Yet like preteens everywhere, his fellow students had guffawed about his African ancestry and made fun of his Indonesian upbringing. The entire first month at Punahou was what Barack Obama later called "a 10-year-old's nightmare."

Despite Hawai'i's reputation as a multicultural, polyglot paradise where the warm, welcoming Aloha Spirit prevailed with the trade winds, it wasn't easy for a *malihini*, or newcomer, to become accepted. This was true in many segments of the population, nowhere more so than among middle school and high school students, who are perhaps the most clique-conscious of all human beings. In his best-selling memoir, the politician Barack Obama described the inner turmoil he experienced as a Punahou student and an outsider in the Islands' mixed white and Asian environment.

In his recollection of his Punahou years, Obama saw himself as a young man filled with angst, searching without an understanding guide to understand what it was to be black in America. Yet his classmates would remember him 30 years later as a normal kid, a little on the shy side, but a regular guy, funny and warm, with a playful sense of humor. "He was a good kid, affable, smiling, happy-go-lucky," said Eldredge. Some classmates believed that his angst was more the product of having been left by his parents to live with his grandparents than anything having to do with his search for ethnic identity or being born of mixed blood. As a young person looking to fill the void left by a missing parent, he was probably a lot more like other Hawai'i kids than he knew.

Growing up in Hawai'i in the '70s as he did, or living in Hawai'i in the '60s when his parents met, it was impossible not to be touched by the unique interracial, intercultural human environment that was Hawai'i's gift to the world. In 1999, before he gave words to his philosophy of national unity, Barack Obama wrote in the Punahou School *Bulletin*: "I realize how truly lucky I am to have been raised here. Hawai'i's spirit of tolerance might not have been perfect, but it was—and is—real. The opportunity that Hawai'i offered, to experience a variety of cultures in a climate of mutual respect, became an integral part of my worldview and a basis for the values I hold most dear." ⨯

CHAPTER THREE

"WHERE NO ONE SEEMS CONSCIOUS OF COLOR"
HAWAI'I IN THE TIME OF STATEHOOD

Barry Obama's father was born half a world away from Hawai'i. Far from all land masses, farther than any populated area is from any continent, the Hawaiian Islands lie anchored in the middle of the world's largest ocean. Hawai'i's antipode—the place that is just opposite Hawai'i if you could dig straight through the earth—is the South African republic of Botswana, which isn't far from Kenya. The man who would be Barry's father left Nairobi on a chartered flight filled with scholarship students who would fan out across the United States. He would be the only African scholarship student in Hawai'i. The year was 1959, a remarkable year in Hawai'i's remarkable history. It was a year that would transform Hawai'i virtually overnight from a backwater tropical territory to a vibrant, growing state full of promise that was destined to reshape the very idea of what an American state could be.

A year earlier, pro-Statehood activists were irritated when political horse-trading put sparsely populated Alaska ahead of the Islands in the race for the 49th star. It was a strategy designed to end run the complex of anti-Statehood objections—real or imagined—that always cropped up when Hawai'i was packaged with Alaska as an all-or-nothing deal. There were a number of "reasons" why Hawai'i should not join the Union: It was non-contiguous, travel time from the Islands to Washington would be onerous, and so forth. Absurd. Equally absurd, but far more compelling at the time, were fears that Communists controlled the territory's labor unions. *Do we want an agent from Moscow sitting in Congress?* And above all were questions of race and ethnicity. Many in Congress, including some who would later become staunch supporters of Statehood, feared admitting a state that would be dominated by non-whites. It was Hawai'i's very "otherness," its special mix and diversity that are today a source of such great pride for candidate Obama and for his home state, that was most troubling.

Former segregationist Senator J. Strom Thurmond of South Carolina, who as it turned out fathered his own mixed-race child, captured the race fear during one of the many statehood debates: "There are many shades and mixtures of heritages in the world," Thurmond would say, "but there are only two extremes. Our society may well be said to be, for the present at least, the exemplification of the maximum development of the Western civilization, culture and heritage. At the opposite extreme exists the Eastern heritage, different in every essential—not necessarily inferior, but different as regards the very thought processes within the individuals who comprise the resultant society." And as was often the case during such arguments, Thurmond dragged out Rudyard Kipling:

"As one of the most competent, and certainly the most eloquent, interpreters of the East to the West, Rudyard Kipling felt the bond of love of one for the other; but at the same time he had the insight to express the impassable difference with the immortal words, 'East is East and West is West and never the twain shall meet,'" Thurmond concluded ponderously and, as time would tell, most inaccurately. Hawai'i might have been the first state with a non-white majority, but it would not be the last. Today, several states have non-white majorities. By mid-century, demographers say, the United States as a whole will be majority non-white.

The Alaska-first strategy proved to be wise. It answered lingering questions about a non-contiguous state, and it sealed the vital support of key congressmen such as Texans Senator Lyndon Johnson and House Speaker Sam Rayburn, who balanced their lingering Southern concerns about Hawai'i's non-white residents with the thought that they would be reliably Democratic voters. With Alaska in, momentum was unstoppable. Hawai'i would be a state. At the time, the idea seemed universally popular, and the party began in earnest on March 13, 1959. That's when word was flashed from Washington that the Hawai'i Statehood Bill had passed Congress. The Royal Hawaiian Band played "Hawai'i Pono'i" (which had once been a national anthem of the Kingdom of Hawai'i), bells rang out, a holiday was declared and a massive bonfire was lit on O'ahu's Sand Island. Five days later, President Dwight D. Eisenhower signed an Admission instrument that called for residents to vote in a plebiscite. In July, Hawai'i went to the polls for the first time as U.S. citizens, overwhelmingly approving Statehood. They elected a 38-year-old Republican governor, an ebullient Mainland transplant named William Quinn. Quinn would be Hawai'i's first and last Republican governor for four decades, until 2002. The Statehood voters also chose a slate of lawmakers that included Democratic Congressman Daniel K. Inouye, a World War II hero who had fought with the famed 442nd Infantry Battalion in Europe. Inouye would serve alongside Barack Obama in the U.S. Senate nearly half a century later. Inouye's meteoric rise as a public servant accompanied the post-war power grab that made Americans of Japanese ancestry by most accounts the most successful patch in the patchwork quilt of Hawai'i's political and social fabric. Central to the excitement of 1959 was the day when Hawai'i, a former kingdom, republic and territory, would actually be admitted as the last state to enter the Union. That happened on August 21, when Eisenhower finally signed the Admission Bill.

Only later would the misgivings of some Native Hawaiians become public. For some Hawaiians, Statehood was nothing to celebrate. It was the last act in the destruction of what had once been an independent nation. But those misgivings were for another day. In 1999, on the 40th anniversary of Statehood, a group of Hawaiians gathered at historic 'Iolani Palace, site of the 1893 overthrow, to protest Statehood and issue a proclamation declaring that, from their point of view, the 1959 Statehood process was "a fraud."

But for most people, at least in those heady optimistic days of 1959, Statehood was indeed cause for celebration. In a quote that was to become famous, whether or not it had actually been uttered, a young man is supposed to have said: "Today, we are all *haoles*." These new citizens were a distinctly different breed of American. A census was underway that would paint a portrait of this new state quite unlike any other in the Union. These new Americans were young. The median age of the 632,000 or so residents was an astonishing 24 years old. Nearly 40 percent were under 18, not yet even old enough to vote. And these new Americans were diverse in ways the rest of the United States had never seen. More than two-thirds of Hawai'i's residents were non-white, an amazing mix of Japanese, Chinese, Filipino, Hawaiian and other races. Just a few thousand were, according to the race classification of the day, Negro.

The political and social impact of all this was contained in a single profound thought that has been the central controlling principle in politics and social relations in the Islands ever since: In Hawai'i, no race is in the majority. The different ethnic groups lived and worked together in quiet neighborhoods with little sign of outward conflict. Even so, Hawai'i was still a society dominated by white, or *haole*, figures who ran the business establishment through an interconnected web of trading, commercial, banking and land companies known as the Big Five. Hawai'i's non-white population, largely the sons and daughters of immigrants who had come to work on the plantations, were beginning to make their move into politics where they dominated the new state Legislature and soon would take over the all-powerful governor's office. But at that time, many recognized that true power still rested for the most part in the hands of the businessmen (and they were mostly men) who ran things from the commercial centers on Bishop Street in downtown Honolulu.

The city's massive building boom was still largely in the planning stages. The tallest building in downtown Honolulu at the time, clearly visible in one memorable scene from the 1961 Elvis Presley movie *Blue Hawaii*, was Aloha Tower, which stood tall above the coconut trees on the waterfront. That scene was shot from Pu'u 'Ualaka'a State Park on Tantalus, a spot that offered panoramic views of the city. The park would later become a favorite picnic spot for Obama's family.

A few months before Statehood became reality, there was big excitement at the old Honolulu Airport, a converted tradewind-cooled Quonset hut with shiny cement floors and faded rattan furniture. Just before noon on July 1, a Qantas 707 airliner set down, bringing Hawai'i officially into the Jet Age and the era of mass tourism. In 1959 there were fewer than 250,000 visitors. Before the Jet Age, visitors came with steamer trunks, tennis rackets and panama hats, and they would linger for weeks, or even months, on the verandah of the pink Royal Hawaiian Hotel. Hawai'i was exclusive, the Palm Springs of the Pacific. All that was about to change. While Qantas had by chance the honor of being first, it was the other airlines—particularly Pan American World Airlines and United—that would promote the Islands as a place every American with an itch for the tropics could reach. Hawai'i was no longer a distant dream.

With Statehood finally in hand, the pace of progress shifted into overdrive. For generations, Hawai'i had operated at a genteel pace, producing sweet sugar cane and pineapple, hosting a trickle of well-heeled tourists and enjoying the payday spending of the soldiers and sailors stationed at the many military bases around O'ahu. Now the demands of mass tourism would lure thousands of workers off the plantations and into the hotels and resorts going up around the Islands. The quiet, structured plantation life was breaking down. A trade class emerged and government expanded. Building a new state almost from scratch required hiring legions of new workers. Their numbers would come from a different generation of local-born residents, a generation that could see beyond a future of plantation work. The sons and daughters of the plantation generation—exposed to the world through military service and with ambitions fueled by education and a modest amount of affluence—were becoming politicians, teachers, nurses, clerks and, as they gained seniority, managers. With money in their pockets and ambitions soaring, Hawai'i's residents began demanding homes. Along with a push for government hiring, the surge of new hotels and residential construction brought with it the good-paying jobs that construction demands. On the site of what had once been swampland on the outskirts of Waikīkī, a vast new shopping center was about to open for business. The $28 million Ala Moana Center opened that summer with 80 shops and parking for 4,000 cars, making it the world's biggest open-air shopping complex. The new shopping center would henceforth be the terminus for city buses, signaling the end of the line for the five-and-dimes and smart shops along Fort Street downtown. It also signaled the maturity of a retail economy in the Islands.

Just as Hawai'i was getting accustomed to the idea of Statehood, a California industrialist by the name of Henry J. Kaiser burst onto the Island scene with big ideas. Kaiser, who had made a fortune in cement and shipbuilding, would transform the sleepy Niumalu Hotel on the outskirts of Waikīkī into the fabulous Hawaiian Village Hotel, a model for the mega-resorts that would follow in later years on Maui and the Big Island. A new state would need a new suburbia, and so Kaiser took aim at some 6,000 acres of scrubby land in East O'ahu, where he would create a sprawling California-like suburb called Hawai'i Kai. In 1958, he opened Kaiser Permanente Hospital, which provided affordable medical care on the model of the old plantation clinics. Around the same time, over on the Big Island of Hawai'i, a volcanic eruption at Kīlauea Iki ended years of dormancy. The Islands were alive, literally exploding and growing from within.

Newcomers to the new state must have wondered, *How did it get to be this way? How is it that Hawai'i is American, but also Hawaiian?*

The first settlers of Hawai'i were Polynesian seafarers who brilliantly navigated thousands of miles of open seas in double-hulled canoes to find a new homeland. In an amazing feat, considering the limited natural resources they found on far-flung islands in the middle of the Pacific, the *kānaka maoli*, or indigenous Hawaiians, organized a perfectly workable way of life that was self-sustaining with what could be grown in the native forests and gathered from the surrounding seas. They understood "sustainability" centuries before the word was coined.

Some centuries later, the *kānaka maoli* were "discovered" by navigators in ships so big by comparison with their tiny canoes that the Hawaiians thought of them as little floating islands. Britain's Captain James Cook, one of many navigators who found their way to Hawai'i, named the archipelago the

Sandwich Islands. This had nothing to do with his hunger and everything to do with Cook's debt to the Earl of Sandwich. First seen by the Native Hawaiians as divine, because his ship's white sails recalled the banners carried in honor of the god Lono, the all-too-human Cook was killed in a huge cross-cultural misunderstanding on St. Valentine's Day 1779. Even without him, his ships returned to Europe and his men let the secret out: The Sandwich Isles possessed astounding beauty and were populated by lithe, handsome people who were pleasing in many ways. Westerners beat a sea path to the Islands, which the American journalist Mark Twain would lovingly call the "loveliest fleet of islands that lays anchored in any sea."

More and more boats moored in the harbors, their crews hungry for fresh food, grog and entertainment. Sailors from as far away as China, Russia, Western Europe, Spanish Mexico and New England poured off these sailing ships, bringing both the good and bad of the developed world: modern technology, tools and weapons, and foreign ideas, pests and diseases. Commerce grew between the Islands and Asia and the far Pacific Northwest, including British Columbia and Alaska. Unknown to the outside world in the 1700s, Hawai'i had become a center of Pacific commerce during the 1800s. In an era when tall ships crisscrossed the Seven Seas, Hawai'i became the Crossroads of the Pacific. The next wave of arrivals included Protestant missionaries from New England, who came to enlighten what they saw as the heathen. They were joined by the rough-hewn whalers of the world, who knew a great port stop when they saw one. When gold was discovered in California in 1848, San Francisco was little more than a collection of tents and shanties while Honolulu was a bustling port city with schools, newspapers and even a theater where opera was performed. Forty-niners would stop to buy provisions en route to the gold fields of California.

In awe of European sailing ships and early technology, the Native Hawaiians welcomed strangers with open arms. In the formative years of the Hawaiian kingdom, the *ali'i*, or chiefs, had no qualms about marrying off ruling-class women to the charismatic adventurers, advisers and entrepreneurs who washed up on Hawai'i's shores. Because Hawaiians cherished children unconditionally, there never was a hint of the Western opprobrium attached to being a "half-breed." The local term *hapa-haole*, meaning "half-white," held no negative connotation in the Kingdom of Hawai'i, and over the years, the term *hapa*, which simply means "half," was applied to individuals of mixed race, no matter which races were combined or if there were more than two ethnic groups contributing to the mix.

The acceptance of cultural and ethnic differences and the combining of them seemed to fit perfectly into the value system of the indigenous people. In modern times their worldview would be given a name, the Aloha Spirit. The word *aloha* itself was defined as the sharing of life and breath, *hā*, with relatives and loved ones. This sharing of breath was expressed in the Hawaiians' greeting, the *honi*, which involved a close nasal embrace and the literal inhaling of each other's breath. But as Native Hawaiian cultural expert Aunty Pilahi Paki has explained, the concept of "aloha" incorporates a handful of values and behavioral traits that conveniently form an acronym for ALOHA: *akahai* (kindness expressed with tenderness), *lōkahi* (unity expressed with harmony), *'olu'olu* (agreeableness expressed with pleasantness), *ha'aha'a* (humility expressed with modesty) and *ahonui* (patience expressed with perseverance.)

Even in ancient times, *aloha* meant taking in family members of blood, adopting others called *hānai* relations and welcoming newcomers into the circle called *'ohana*, or family. Foreigners happily accepted the Native Hawaiians' *aloha* while belittling their backward ways that stood in the way of progress. Before long, Western notions of private land ownership, plantation-style agriculture and the pressing need to make a profit took root in Hawai'i's sun-drenched volcanic soil. It is an often-repeated observation that the missionaries came to do good and ended by doing well, very well, financially, as they and their offspring intermarried with Hawaiian royalty and became land-owning entrepreneurs and captains of industry.

When workers were needed to toil in the plantations set up by the foreigners, the indigenous Hawaiian people found themselves sharing their island oasis with more foreigners: laborers from China, Japan, Portugal, the Philippines, Korea and Puerto Rico. Some said the beauty of plantation-era Hawai'i was not that all the races blended into one, but that Hawai'i's ethnic groups managed to retain their cultural identities in concert with all the others.

The more people Hawai'i welcomed, the more intermarriage there was, and gradually the introduced cultures were mixed with those of the earlier arrivals. People of three, four and more ethnic groups laughingly describe their racial heritage as *chop-suey*, a mixed vegetable and noodle dish, or *poi-dog*, the local name for a mutt or mixed-breed dog. In more modern times, when Hawai'i's reputation as a place where the Golden People of multiple races took root, children who were ethnically unmixed took their parents to task, asking, "Why aren't I part-something else?"

The first push for Hawai'i to become a state came in the 1850s, when

King Kamehameha III entered into secret negotiations that proved to be 100 years before their time. In 1898, the short-lived Republic of Hawai'i, which, after a bloodless revolution in 1893, had replaced the Hawaiian monarchy, was folded to allow for the formal annexation of Hawai'i as a territory of the United States. The federal government took charge and administered Hawai'i like an ugly stepchild. The idea of Statehood was still a slow-starter in the 20th century. Though the Islands had played a strategic role in the Spanish-American War, it took World War II and the attack on Pearl Harbor to validate the geopolitical importance of Hawai'i as a mid-Pacific staging area for the national defense. U.S. military installations on Hawai'i's main island of O'ahu—the Navy's Pearl Harbor, the Army's Schofield Barracks, the Kāne'ohe Marine Corps Air Station and Hickam Air Force Base—proved to be aces in the hole for convincing some congressmen to back Hawai'i's bid for admission into the Union.

During World War II, Hawai'i-born troops of Japanese ancestry had fought hard on the battlefields of Europe to prove their mettle in the defense of America. They came back from the war as some of the most highly decorated heroes of the Great Generation. Though some still encountered discrimination in Hawai'i's booming post-war economy, the AJA veterans also established themselves in business and government to the point where some lines of business seemed locked up by Japanese-Americans and more than half of Hawai'i's state and municipal civil servants were of Japanese ancestry. This predominance in post-war society and their continued cohesiveness as a group, evidenced in the influential Club 100 and 442nd Veterans organizations, eventually translated into enduring political clout. Strangely enough, Hawai'i's post-Statehood political surge coalesced around the persona of a white-haired *haole* ex-cop named John A. Burns, whose Irish working-class ethos won the trust of the AJAs, most of the unions and the other ethnic plantation-based groups. The local Democratic Party rebuilt itself as the well-oiled "Burns Machine" and set out to end Hawai'i's long run of Republican dominance.

Socially, Hawai'i's young people were excitedly exerting their Americanness in a uniquely multicultural environment. Their parents had struggled to retain their tight-knit ethnic communities to keep their cultural traditions alive. They lived by the tacit understanding, *If we Japanese/Chinese/Filipinos/ Koreans/Portuguese are to get ahead, we have to stick together.* In the post-Statehood era, their children were striving to downplay their ethnic identities in order to achieve that near-total WASPy individuality that characterized the core culture of the movies and the television. But the wheel would circle again with the following generation, Barry's generation, which turned once more with pride to its ethnic heritage and special Island identity.

In 1959, the world was not as safe and secure as it seemed from the point of view of Hawai'i. Tension was building in Europe. The Cold War was heating up and firing up nuclear proliferation and the Space Race. What Eisenhower described as the American "military-industrial complex" was rattling its military-industrial sabers. Soon the Berlin Wall would go up, separating Free Europe from Communist Europe. War was simmering in a place called Indochina.

Far from these conflicts, Hawai'i reveled in its new role as a place where East met West, and just as Geneva, Switzerland, was famous for international conferences, Honolulu began to think of itself as the Geneva of the Pacific. In 1960, Congress had set up a program called the East-West Center for Technical and Cultural Interchange. Better known as the East-West Center, for short, it was envisioned as a place where bright young people from Asia would do cooperative research with young Americans. The East-West Center's mandate from Congress was to strengthen relations and understanding among the nations of Asia, the Pacific and the United States, and to promote the development of a stable, prosperous, peaceful Asia Pacific community through cooperative study, education and research. In essence, the new educational institution was something of a Peace Corps in reverse, with talented and skilled foreigners coming to help Americans with their studies. It was hoped that idealistic Asian grantees would enjoy their time in America and go back home to become leaders in their own countries. The Center's buildings, including the I.M. Pei-designed Thomas Jefferson Hall and the modernistic John F. Kennedy Theatre, were adjacent to the campus of the University of Hawai'i at Mānoa, which was becoming a state university and multicultural learning center in its own right.

What better place to make friends for America than Hawai'i, with its beautiful weather, beautiful beaches and equally beautiful tradition of welcoming visitors? Throughout its years of fostering technical and cultural interchange, the East-West Center became known for its social interaction or "interculturation." From the time the East-West Center welcomed its first batch of international scholars in 1961 until now, the Center and the affiliated University of Hawai'i have been places where people of different races and national backgrounds meet. Not surprisingly, given the sunny skies and dispositions, scores of individuals who met there married there.

Into this plumeria-scented air charged with opportunity and hope came a bright, upwardly mobile young man from Nairobi, Barack Obama Senior. The bespectacled African student had done his homework. He arrived in Hawai'i aware of its reputation, fully accepting the idea that Hawai'i represented a new ideal for racial harmony and diversity.

The 23-year-old student had barely settled in that fall when his commanding presence caught the eye of a local gossip columnist: "Barack Obama, a UH student from Kenya, is delighted to find that persons of different racial backgrounds live in harmony here and all consider themselves Americans," the columnist reported. "He's also delighted with the *hula* girls, whose swiveling and swaying [are] akin to the *owalo*, a sort of seldom-seen African *hula*."

Obama clearly wanted to please his hosts and flatter them on their image, real or perceived. The "most surprising thing," he told an interviewer shortly after arriving in the Islands, was the lack of race prejudice. Hawai'i, he observed, has an "inter-racial attitude where no one seems to be conscious of color." Years later, explaining the complex story of his birth, the African student's son, another Barack Obama, who graduated from Harvard Law School, said he was born of parents who began life on two different continents and met in Hawai'i. Like so many young people who chose to mingle with people from other countries, they shared a common dream of lasting peace. His parents shared what he called "an improbable love," which would not last. And though neither was religious, they shared a faith in the goodness and potential of humankind, which would somehow live on in their son.

Barack Senior cut an imposing figure on the tree-lined campus of the University of Hawai'i. Wanting to fit in, he chose "Barry" as his American name. His skin was a rich ebony, the color of deep-roasted coffee, and he wore thick black plastic eyeglasses that marked him as an intellectual. He spoke in a deep voice with a clipped British accent. People who saw him were reminded of the singer Nat King Cole, who was the first black American to have his own television show. Today they might think of the actors Sidney Poitier or James Earl Jones. Those who met the bespectacled Barack Senior found him self-assured and opinionated. He was a talker who possessed a powerful, persuasive personality. After speaking with him awhile, you would discover that the foreign student who had come to Hawai'i to study economics was very ambitious and very determined to succeed. He would not go back to Africa as anything less than an economist with a high degree of education and the diplomas to prove it. He was not only a talker but a doer. Newly arrived as a foreign student, he organized an International Student Association at UH and became its first president. Without a family in Hawai'i, he lived at the Atherton YMCA on University Avenue opposite the UH campus until he married and moved in with the woman who would be Barry Junior's mother.

This was Stanley Ann Dunham, who had graduated from a Seattle-area high school in 1960. Her dream was to attend the University of Chicago, which had accepted her on early admission, but her father, Stan Dunham, made it clear that Chicago was not an option. She was far too young and inexperienced. Her second choice would have been to remain in Seattle and attend the University of Washington, but as fate would have it, her father was offered a job in Hawai'i, which was becoming superheated by the political, social and economic lava flow that was Statehood. Stanley Junior didn't want to move to Honolulu, but her father, Stanley Senior, got his way.

The University of Hawai'i, perched directly behind Waikīkī, was a quiet place in those days. Built as an original Land Grant college, the university was the first and only serious choice for Island-born students who could not afford, or were unwilling, to travel to the mainland United States. In 1960, the tranquil campus of the University of Hawai'i at Mānoa was not known for political activism, or any type of activism, for that matter, other than the act of heading for the beaches after class. The Vietnam War would nearly be over before anti-war demonstrations broke out on the Mānoa campus. Yet in its own quiet way, UH was stirring with the first signs of internationalism, striving to be a place where academics and students from East and West could meet, study and take their place in the world.

As it happened, Barack Obama Senior and Ann Dunham, as she was called, born half a world apart, enrolled in the same Russian-language class. It was not the kind of class that most students in Hawai'i were clamoring to take, but it was a testament to the geopolitical awareness of the black man from Africa and the white woman from Seattle that they signed up for it. The two scholars had friends in common, including a burly crew-cut graduate student from Buffalo, New York, named Neil Abercrombie, who had also been drawn to the exotic new state. They became part of a foreign and like-minded student clique that talked and talked, solved the world's problems, drank beer and listened to jazz. In the tradition of Hawai'i's myriad mixed-race love stories, Ann and Barack Senior fell in love over a matter of months and vowed to marry, against all odds, disregarding what other people might think about their unlikely match.

In the early '60s, change began blowing in the wind. In Africa, Kenya was on the verge of gaining its independence from Britain, at the head of a queue of countries getting ready to lift the mantle of European colonialism from the enormous continent. In America, the surprise election of John F. Kennedy promised a New Frontier, and the Peace Corps was encouraging young Americans to make the world a better place by digging wells and helping to educate and empower individuals who could then build communities and nations. Back at home, black performers had emerged from the shadows into the entertainment mainstream, so that it was acceptable for a man named Chubby Checker to teach children and adults to do the Twist, getting them to move in sexually suggestive ways Elvis never did. The civil rights movement was moving ahead, with dramatic demands for a final end to racial segregation in the South. Though things were changing in the early '60s, most Americans were not prepared to see or accept interracial couples.

As Barack Obama pointed out in *Dreams*, black-white marriage was still against the law in several states when his parents met in 1961. In fact, miscegenation, defined as sexual relations or marriage between races, was illegal in 16 states, though not in Hawai'i. Half a century after the Civil War, in 1912, opposition to mixed-race marriage was keen. Southern lawmakers spearheaded a drive for an Amendment to the Constitution that would have criminalized the love of two people if they happened to be black and white. Ironically, the Anti-Miscegenation Amendment would have been the Sixteenth Amendment, following the Fifteenth, which forbids the government from using a citizen's race, color or previous status as a slave as a qualification for voting. In proposing the amendment, Senator Seaborn A. Roddenberry of Georgia argued passionately that "intermarriage between whites and blacks is repulsive and averse to every sentiment of pure American spirit. It is abhorrent and repugnant. It is subversive to social peace. It is destructive of moral supremacy, and ultimately this slavery to black beasts will bring this nation to a fatal conflict," he said, calling on Congress to "uproot and exterminate now this debasing, ultra-demoralizing, un-American and inhuman leprosy."

The constitutional amendment to federalize the crime drew little support, but state "racial integrity" laws aimed at keeping the races apart remained in effect for decades to come. In the socially complacent Eisenhower years, theatre-goers were shocked or delighted at the theme of the 1949 Rodgers and Hammerstein musical *South Pacific*, based on stories by Hawai'i's James A. Michener. A pivotal point of the story centers on a crisis of the heart that comes when the sweet U.S. Navy nurse Nellie Forbush, of Little Rock, Arkansas, discovers that her fiancé, the French planter Emil deBecque, has mixed-race children from a previous marriage to a Polynesian woman. At the same time, the story's hero, Lt. Joe Cable, falls for a local girl against a background of racial bigotry when children have been carefully taught "before they were six, seven or eight / To hate the people their parents hate." When the story resurfaced as a feature film in 1958, the topic of mixed-marriage romance was still sensitive. Even in the era of Kennedy's Camelot, many Americans from the Bible Belt to the Pacific Coast believed that the mixing of the black and white races was against God's will.

In 1963, Virgina Judge Leon Bazile upheld a Virginia court ruling banning a black-white couple from living together as man and wife in the Dominion State, writing: "Almighty God created the races white, black, yellow, Malay and red, and he placed them on separate continents.... The fact that he separated the races shows that he did not intend for the races to mix." On June 12, 1967, the U.S. Supreme Court overturned the Virginia law and banned anti-miscegenation laws throughout the land.

A decade after *South Pacific* and about a year before Barack Senior met Ann Dunham, the groundbreaking film *Guess Who's Coming to Dinner* was playing on movie screens across America. In the Academy Award-winning drama, the characters played by Spencer Tracy and Katharine Hepburn are shaken to their core when their daughter introduces them to her fiancé, whom she has met in, of all places, Hawai'i. Her intended is a brilliant black doctor, played by Sidney Poitier. At one point, the daughter explains: "It never occurred to me that I would fall in love with a Negro, but I have, and nothing's going to change that." Later, her gruff father obligingly observes: "You're two wonderful people who happened to fall in love and happen to have a pigmentation problem." The Sidney Poitier character notes matter-of-factly that "a lot of people are going to see us as a shocking pair."

To this day, interracial marriage remains relatively rare on the Mainland, where it is estimated that only about seven percent of America's 59 million marriages unite individuals of different races. However in Hawai'i, for reasons of history and culture, mixed-race marriages were not that unusual even in the '60s; in fact, they were becoming the norm. As a result of immigration from East and West and interracial marriages, more than 20 percent of Hawai'i residents identify themselves as being of "Two or More Races"—a number that undoubtedly undercounts those of mixed blood who choose to identify with one ethnicity over another. The most common racial designation for children born in the state today is "mixed." More than half of all births nowadays fall into that category. "Hawai'i is leading the nation in seeing what America will become," said Alvin Onaka, the state Registrar of Vital Statistics. But a black-white couple was not a common sight on the streets of Honolulu, where the percentage of Africans and African Americans is minuscule compared with the Polynesian, Asian and European American populations. Even with Hawai'i's high degree of tolerance, Barack Senior and Ann Dunham Obama were most certainly seen as a shocking pair. ⟨⟩

CHAPTER FOUR

"White as milk, black as pitch"
A Woman from America, a Man from Africa

He was a small chubby baby born in Honolulu, a community well known for its blend of Polynesian, Asian-American and mixed-race children. His parents were none of the above: a white American-born woman and black African-born man. Of his early childhood, Barack Obama Junior would write: "My father looked nothing like the people around me. That he was black as pitch, my mother white as milk, barely registered in my mind." His pale-skinned mother once told him that he had inherited his eyebrows from her but his character and his brilliant mind from his father. Looking back at the mother and grandparents who raised Barry (who also took his father's nickname), his half-sister Maya observed that Barry was "the perfect combination of them all": his impulsive, iconoclastic, humanist mother; his pragmatic, businesslike maternal grandmother, who typified the bank escrow officer she was; and his grandfather, an impetuous, itinerant furniture salesman who had a way with people and yearned to be a poet.

Although Barack Obama's first book was called *Dreams from My Father*, his father's direct influence on him was little more than that, a dream. This was a father whom Barry never truly knew. The actual time they spent together was extremely limited. As a little boy, Barry grew up without his father's presence. As a child, he said, he was as unaware that he was supposed to have a live-in father as he was that he was supposed to have a racial designation. At age 10, he would spend one uncomfortable month with Barack Senior, and as a young man he would only know his father from the formal letters he exchanged with and visits he made to his father's family in Kenya after his father's death, so that he could discover his Obama roots.

From his father's blood he inherited the soul of Africa, and everything that means in America. From his mother, he inherited the rest of the world, in the form of her yearning to get close to people of all kinds; to help the downtrodden rise up; to develop their potential for the greater global good. In fact, Barack Obama owes far more of his personality and political philosophy to his mother, who provided the life lessons, the guidance and advice that fashioned him in her mold as an internationalist and a passionate and free-thinking liberal. It was only later in his life, after his father's death and in the months before his mother's death, that Barack Obama began to appreciate what a profound and positive influence his mother had had on him and how she had helped put him on a path to change America.

The unusual couple took pleasure in defying convention and raining consternation on their family and friends. Each had come to Hawai'i with a family history of defiance, ambition and courage behind them. To understand them, one must appreciate how far they had come, geographically and philosophically, from their small-town roots in the middle of Africa and the middle of America.

Barry Junior's grandfather, Hussein Onyango Obama, was born in 1895, when Kenya was still an African jewel in the crown of the British Empire. Onyango's life, between 1895 and 1975, coincided with the transformation of Kenya from a traditional tribal society into an independent nation facing the challenges of development. As the Obama family story goes, Onyango, who was of the Luo ethnic group, was the first person from their village to actually see a white man. When he returned from a visit to the provincial capital of Kisumu, he shocked the village by wearing the first trousers, shirt and shoes they had ever seen. Seeing a Luo draped in such strange clothing frightened the adults and made the children cry.

In the early part of the 20th century, few Luo could read or write the white man's language. Onyango was one of them. Few villagers could afford to ride the train, and so when he went off to seek work in Nairobi, Onyango walked. It was a two-week journey by foot. Along the way he was confronted by leopards and snakes and was chased up a tree by a belligerent water buffalo. In Nairobi, he found work supervising road crews, and later cooking and cleaning in British homes. He learned the ways of Kenya's colonial masters, who praised him for his ability to read and write English, follow recipes and make pastry. On the one hand, he admired their machines, their medicine and the social organization they had built by putting God and king before individual and family concerns. He observed that the white man is like an ant that can be easily crushed; but working together in order and harmony, ants can move mountains. On the other hand, he saw that the British were class-conscious among their own and race-conscious as overseers of Africa.

With the wages he earned, he bought land and cattle in his family's native place, Kendu, and when he returned to live there, the villagers were astounded by his resolve to keep his house, his food and his children spot-lessly clean. He was at once modern and traditional, believing that the best way for Africa was the African way. There is a photograph of him in a pris-tine, stiffly starched white shirt and a *kanga*, a man's skirt. Across his lap is a huge club wrapped in animal skin.

When World War II broke out, he went to work for the British Army as a cook in the service of a captain, who took him to Burma and Ceylon and other outposts of the British Empire. Though respected for his skill, he was called "Boy" by his employers for most of his life. After the war, Onyango used his wits and the experience he gained from working with British colo-nials and applied them once again to farming. He settled in Alego, a poor village in Nyanza Province on the shores of Lake Victoria, the largest lake in Africa, on land his grandfather had abandoned. Onyango took the unusual step of selling off valuable cattle to make the land more productive for cash crops like bananas, mangoes and papayas. He kept goats, which his sons would tend. Apart from being a successful farmer, Onyango was a much-respected elder of the Luo tribe, the predominant ethnic group along the lake. He was known for his word. What he said, he did. He respected strength and the discipline of tribal life. He was also a modern man who rejected notions of the past if they went against science and what was needed for a country to progress. He could advise villagers on how to cure ailments with herbal medicines, but he once had a run-in with a man who sold magic potions and curses. He tried to be a Christian but rejected that religion because it was too forgiving. He was one of the first Luo in his district to embrace Islam. Having seen what the British could do, he was keenly aware of the value of formal education for boys, yet he stubbornly believed that paying out school fees for girls was a waste of time.

Barack Onyango Obama was his third child and one of whom he was especially fond, not for his beauty but for his brains. Barack was born with an appetite and an aptitude for education. While still a child, he learned to read and write better than his father. He was mindful of the Old Man when his father was around, but he was born with a bent toward mischief-mak-ing. When his father came back from business trips, villagers would tell him that little Barack had been seen wrestling here, riding someone's cattle there, swimming somewhere he shouldn't. Barack attended a mud-walled mission school in his village but was too advanced for it. The next closest school was six miles away, and he would walk there every day to learn what he could from the man who taught there. There too he found himself too advanced.

On occasion he would speak up in front of the whole class to correct his teacher's mistakes, and for this insolence he was, beaten by the teacher with a thick bamboo rod. That prompted him to change schools again, and again he found the curriculum too easy. He could learn a month's worth of lessons in days, and even if he skipped school for days, his test scores were usually perfect. The local schools bored him. Few Luo obtained secondary education in those days, but he passed an entrance examination and was admitted to the Maseno Mission School, about 50 miles from his home.

The teachers at Maseno recognized the teenaged Obama for his brilliant mind but also for his brand of mischief and his propensity for breaking school rules. Before long, he was expelled. When Onyango learned of this, he sent his son to the port city of Mombasa to find work.

The young man moved from job to job and from Mombasa to Nairobi. Though he was universally regarded as charming and intelligent, he would suffer for his boastfulness and intellectually superior attitude. These were traits his schoolmates at Maseno and peers in the Kenyan bureaucracy would remember years later. Indeed, one of his peers who later became an influential journalist in Nairobi would describe him in later life as "imperious, cruel and given to boasting about his brain and his wealth."

In the late 1950s, Nairobi was lively with political meetings and demonstrations aimed at ousting the colonial power. The anti-British movement, in time to become known as the Mau-Mau Rebellion, caused the British to impose a state of emergency, which was still in place when Barack left on his journey to America. Although the young village intellectual was not a Kikuyu, the dominant group in the uprising, he was attracted to the movement. His peripheral involvement led to a brief arrest by the British. Eventually he found work in a Nairobi office as a clerk. Not wanting to remain a lowly clerk for better-educated Kenyans, and desirous of keeping up with his secondary-school peers, he realized he would need a college education. Because Kenya had no university of its own at the time, the nation's most promising scholars were sent to study at Makarere University in Uganda. Many of Barack's classmates from Maseno were studying there.

He was already 21 years old and did not have a high school diploma when he had a stroke of luck. Two American women, one from California, the other from Maryland, fell into conversation with him at the office where he worked. They told him that with his English skills he could take a correspondence course that would qualify him to take a high school equivalency exam. If he passed that test at the U.S. Embassy in Nairobi, they would help him get into an American college. He studied diligently, completed the course in quick time, passed the test and began writing to American colleges, telling of his desire to help free his country from the mantle of colonialism. The two American women wrote letters of recommendation that helped the charismatic Kenyan gain admission to the University of Hawai'i. Being admitted to UH enabled him to gain a coveted place in a new scholarship program.

According to the *Washington Post*, the Kenyan nationalist Tom Mboya had raised enough money with the help of the African American Students Foundation to bring some of his more promising countrymen to the States to study. Barack Obama Senior would be one of the lucky ones to get a ticket, and with financial assistance from the California woman, noted international literacy campaigner Elizabeth Mooney Kirk, he was given a golden opportunity to obtain higher education. Among the donors to the African American Students Foundation in its first year, 1959, were entertainers Harry Belafonte and Sidney Poitier, and America's first black baseball star, Jackie Robinson. Though the U.S. State Department had originally opposed Mboya's efforts to provide scholarships for Kenyan students, support later came from the Kennedy family and, for later students, from the Kennedy Administration, which sought to win the hearts and minds of Africa as the Cold War made its way to that continent.

Barack Senior left Nairobi in September 1959 with a planeload of 80 other Kenyan students eager to earn a degree in the United States and then return home to help Kenya advance under self-rule. That was how he came to land in Hawai'i, in the middle of the Pacific Ocean. He was the first student from his district to study outside the confines of East Africa and the first to fly on an airplane. He would gain the higher education he sought but would never rise to the position of prominence he saw for himself in his homeland. Before he would return to Kenya, though, he would marry two white American women. The first of them was Stanley Ann Dunham, whom he met not long after he arrived in Honolulu.

In college and her later professional life, Barry's mother was known as Ann. As a child in Wichita, Kansas, she was teased because her given name was Stanley. Her grade-school classmates called her Stan the Man. Barry's grandfather, the man he called Gramps, was named Stanley Armour Dunham. Gramps had wanted a son he could name Stanley Junior. So when his wife, Madelyn, gave birth to a daughter, he named her Stanley Ann. She would later complain to her friends that her father had "wanted a boy, but he got me."

The Dunhams hadn't had an easy life in the gritty hardscrabble oil towns of Kansas. Stanley Dunham came from a working-class family in El Dorado and had gone out as a teenager to find work in the rough days of the Depression when money was scarce and jobs were hard to find. He had toiled as a farm hand and an oil field worker in the 1920s when Kansas was a major oil-producing region.

Madelyn's parents, the Paynes, were middle-class Methodists who lived a dozen or so miles away in Augusta. They were the kind of people who spent their lives striving for respectability. They went to church regularly and ordered the *Great Books of the Western World* series to put on their bookshelf. They didn't go for drinking or dancing, and they didn't go for Stanley, a boisterous Baptist who seemed footloose and fancy-free, not the kind of boy who would settle down to manage oil leases and feed a family as Madelyn's father had done.

For her part, young Madelyn fashioned herself as a modern girl of the '30s. Big band music and swing dancing were becoming popular, and she liked to go into Wichita's Blue Moon club to dance to the music of famed bandleaders like Tommy Dorsey, Benny Goodman and Glenn Miller. Though she came from Scottish-English forebears, Madelyn liked to tell people that her ancestors had been anti-slavery activists in the 1800s and that she had some Cherokee Indian blood. Though he worked as a laborer, Stanley Dunham was a charming, outgoing, talkative type who was destined to be a salesman. A high school friend of his said Stanley could "charm the legs off a couch." Madelyn married Stanley secretly while she was still in high school and still living at home. She didn't tell her parents that she and Stanley were husband and wife until she graduated in June 1940.

On the day after the attack on Pearl Harbor plunged the United States into World War II, Stanley enlisted in the U.S. Army. The Dunhams lived at Fort Leavenworth, where Stanley was stationed. Stanley Ann was born there on November 29, 1942. Before long, Stanley Senior was shipped off to join General George Patton's U.S. Seventh Army. He saw plenty of Europe, though he never saw combat. His young wife stayed behind and worked on the assembly line, a Rosie the Riveter in a Boeing factory that was churning out B-29 bombers. After the war, the young couple struggled to make ends meet back in El Dorado. Madelyn worked in restaurants, while Stanley managed a furniture store on Main Street. He took advantage of the G.I. Bill to take some college courses at the University of California, Berkeley, but he was eager to make money, and the trio soon moved back to Kansas, and then to Texas, where Stanley got back into the furniture business.

In their Texas town, they encountered the kind of Jim Crow mentality that taught Americans that blacks were not entitled to be treated on an equal footing with whites. Even little Stanley Ann met with the wrath of her white neighbors when she made the mistake of playing with a black girl her age. When Madelyn, now known as Toot, told this story to Barry Junior, she said she and Gramps had left Texas because they believed that everyone should be treated decently.

In 1955, the Dunhams moved to Seattle, where Stanley—Gramps to be—had lined up a job with a big furniture store downtown and Madelyn found work as an escrow officer at a suburban bank. Seattle was booming, thanks to Boeing, and bustling middle-class suburbs were sprouting out of the evergreen forests. Stanley Ann Dunham is almost always described in media accounts and by her son as a woman from Kansas. She was born there, it is true, but her spirit was born in the state of Washington, where she was educated through high school. In the classic movie *The Wizard of Oz,* young Dorothy awakens to a world of new sights and shapes, looks around her with wide eyes, and tells her dog: "We're not in Kansas anymore, Toto." Somewhere between junior high school in Kansas and her freshman year at the University of Hawai'i, Stanley Ann Dunham must have had a Dorothy-like realization, waking up and finding that things had changed.

An awkward, porcelain-skinned, dark-haired girl with big thoughtful eyes, Stanley Ann awoke in her teen years to find she was no longer a Midwesterner. She had transformed herself into a young woman of the Northwest. The transformation occurred at about the same time that Seattle was embracing modernity and technology and its future role as a Pacific Rim, indeed a world, city.

Stanley Ann was a 13-year-old eighth-grader when the Dunhams joined the exodus to the suburbs. They chose a sprawling apartment complex on Mercer Island, so that Stanley Ann could thrive in the fresh air of a progressive new high school. In 1955, Mercer Island was a woodsy, overwhelmingly white suburb situated on five acres. To reach the community, motorists exited from a highway, now part of Interstate 90, that carried cars across Lake Washington to and from the bigger suburb of Bellevue. (Unlike its reputation at the time as a modest, middle-class community, Mercer Island today is a tony refuge of the ultra-rich, including Microsoft co-founder Paul Allen.)

It has been said that America was happy in the Eisenhower years, from 1952 to 1960. Despite some early fear about where technology was taking the world, America's middle class seemed satisfied with the cookie-cutter conformity that went hand in hand with political conservatism. The prevailing social sentiment was exalted by milquetoast broadcast media typified by the TV sitcom *Father Knows Best*, in which the father, played by Robert Young, always did know what was best for his family.

The Dunhams of Kansas were probably comfortable with the ultra-square sentiment of the Eisenhower Era, but Stanley Ann became a Beatnik-era cultural rebel. At age 13, she had a notion of what she wanted for America socially and politically. It is interesting to note that in the election of 1956, a Republican was running on a platform of stability, national security and extensive personal experience, while the Democratic challenger was an idealistic U.S. senator from Illinois. Stanley Ann was drawn to Adlai Stevenson, the Democrat positioned as a candidate of change against the incumbent Eisenhower. Stevenson called for "A New America" that would ensure freedom for all regardless of race, creed or economic condition. His best argument against Eisenhower's re-election was that it would benefit the rich and not the average American. These ideas must have appealed to Stanley Ann, who would spend her life helping less fortunate people secure the economic benefits that freedom and equality could bring.

Like a typical bobby-soxer, she confided in close friends that she didn't like the way she looked and complained about her father's domineering *Father Knows Best* personality. On the other hand, she scandalized the others by telling them she was not interested in the traditional female developmental roles of babysitting, dating, getting married and having children. Years before Seattle was celebrated as the birthplace of Starbucks, Stanley Ann was a coffee-shop kind of girl with a quick wit, a wry sense of humor and sarcasm, and a well-developed social consciousness. Her high school friends saw her as strong-willed and unconventional, a free-thinker who challenged ideas that other students accepted without thinking. Classmates remembered her as the kind of person who would ponder weighty questions that no one else would: Is democracy good? What's wrong with Communism? Is there a God? She was encouraged along this progressive path by high school teachers who gave her books with challenging themes and often radical ideas. Two Mercer Island High School teachers in particular gave such out-of-the-ordinary, eyebrow-raising assignments in philosophy and literature, urging discussion of such hush-hush topics as socialism and homosexuality, that the hallway between their classrooms was called "Anarchy Alley."

Had there been such a category, her classmates might have voted Stanley Ann the Class Atheist and the student Most Likely to Succeed at Anti-American Activities. Even so, she went with her parents to the Unitarian Church in Bellevue. The universalistic Unitarian approach to religion was her father's idea, because, he said, you get five religions in one. In later life, Ann would say she was not an atheist; she was open to the thoughts and philosophies of all religions, but she did not affiliate herself with any of them.

Hawai'i was a good place for someone curious about world religions and cultural practices. Christian missionaries had arrived in the Islands in the 1820s, and Catholics had begun their search for converts a scant seven years later. But if the missionaries had a profound impact on Hawai'i, so did immigration, beginning in the 1850s with the importation of Chinese workers. A century later, Christian sects, including the United Church of Christ, Assemblies of God and Southern Baptists, when combined accounted for a majority of churchgoers, while the largest single religious group was the Catholic Church, followed by the Church of Jesus Christ of Latter-day Saints. There were some 70 Buddhist congregations, as well as Jewish, Muslim and Hindu centers of worship. But about 64 percent of Hawai'i's population, like Stanley Ann Dunham, did not identify as part of any organized religion.

In the summer of 1960, the Dunhams settled into a comfortably large house near the Mānoa campus. Stanley Ann, known now as Ann, was 17 going on 18 when she started class at UH in the fall. She had rebelled against her father's attempts to rule her roost and was intellectually, though not financially, emancipated from her parents.

She had talked to them about her boyfriend, Barry. Then one night in 1960, in a replay of the *Guess Who's Coming to Dinner* script, Ann announced her engagement and introduced them to Barack "Barry" Obama. Though they were not shocked by Ann's choice of a boyfriend, Madelyn and Stanley were not pleased. Even though they had become accustomed to multiracial Honolulu, and even though they had come to accept and appreciate her boyfriend as an intelligent and amusing young man, the Dunhams did not welcome the news that Ann planned to marry an African. They had witnessed racial discrimination firsthand and feared, as had Sidney Poitier's character, that the union of black and white would make life more difficult than it needed to be. Barack Obama Junior later said the announcement of his mother's engagement to his father was "not easy to swallow."

But the stubborn, star-crossed lovers seemed intent to wed under Hawai'i's star-filled skies. Word got back to Nairobi that the Dunhams were threatening to get Barack Senior expelled from the university. Barack Senior wrote to his father, urging him to help save the situation. Nonetheless, Onyango Obama sent a "long, nasty letter" to the Dunhams to say he did not want Obama blood "sullied" by marriage to a white woman. To his son he offered a different but equally cutting objection. "How can you marry this white woman when you have responsibilities at home?" he asked. Among those responsibilities were his pregnant Luo wife and the son he had left behind.

Gramps and Toot eventually consented, but grudgingly. Despite their parents' misgivings, no matter how heartfelt, nothing could keep them apart. Barack Senior and Stanley Ann married in February 1961. Neither was religious—Barack Senior was a devout atheist—so there was no church, no minister, no white dress and no big reception. Describing his parents' wedding in *Dreams from My Father*, Obama wrote: "How and when the marriage took place remains a bit murky." He imagined that it was performed by a justice of the peace, although that nomenclature is not used in Hawai'i. Indeed, no marriage license has been located, and during the presidential campaign there was speculation that the wedding of Barack Senior and Stanley Ann was a marriage of faith and conviction rather than a legal marriage. Even murkier, in terms of U.S. law, was Obama Senior's earlier "village marriage" in Kenya to a woman named Kezia, who bore him two children.

To the astonishment of her friends back in Mercer Island, Stanley Ann sent word that she had married the young African. Six months after the marriage, Barack Hussein Obama Junior entered the world, weighing in at 8 pounds, 2 ounces. He was born on August 4, 1961—almost exactly a year after Statehood—at Queen Kapi'olani Hospital for Women and Children, where a significant number of children are born of mixed race, but relatively few of black and white parents.

On Barry's birth certificate, his mother's race is listed as Caucasian and his father's, somewhat oddly, as "African," not a race but a geographic description. In an earlier era, when the Territorial Bureau of Vital Statistics held sway over birth certificates, Barry's race at birth likely would have been described as "Caucasian," as it was the practice to describe children by their mother's race or ethnicity. As if to underscore his uniqueness, Barry's parents gave him the East African name Barack, which means "blessed" in Arabic. The name shares the same linguistic root as the Hebrew name Baruch, also "blessed." The English version of the name is Benedict, and in Spanish it is Benito.

Living in Mānoa Valley close to the mountains and the sea, the Obamas and the Dunhams were like any other 'ohana who hiked up to waterfalls nestled in the mountaintop rainforest and made regular trips to the beach.

Gramps and Toot facilitated these outings, and they were the cement that held the family together in Hawai'i.

In some of the family snapshots, Little Barry is playing on the shore of Waikīkī, riding a tricycle, swinging a baseball bat bigger than he is. He looks as happy as any child could be. If Hawai'i was in any way a paradise, it was a paradise for kids growing up barefoot and carefree.

If you grew up in Hawai'i as Barry did, and tried to enumerate the things that made living there so special, you might begin by stating the obvious: You see the ocean every day; it is a constant, as old as life on Earth, yet it changes every day. You're never far from a waterfall, a V-shaped valley or a rainforest. You can wear sunglasses every day and at the same time carry an umbrella against the sun or the showers that hover over the mountain slopes. In Hawai'i, the seasons announce themselves far more subtly than on the Mainland, though you know when spring comes because the big surf switches from the North Shore to Waikīkī and the South Shore. You know it is summer when the mangoes and lychee on backyard trees turn red and luscious. You know when it was winter because humpback whales frolic in the channels between the Islands, and the kōlea, the bird known as the golden plover, arrive all skinny from Alaska to stilt-walk on your lawn, and the surf on the North Shore is so huge it threatens to come up onto the highway. Hawaiians celebrate all the American holidays and their own Kūhio Day, Kamehameha Day and Admission Day, as well as traditional cultural observances including Chinese New Year, Boys Day, Girls Day and the O-bon season. Many of Hawai'i's people celebrate every weekend as an excuse to stay out of doors, having a picnic under a blue tarp at a beach park, cooking and eating, inviting family and friends for a potluck, surfing, fishing, swimming, snorkeling, diving, windsurfing, hiking, sailing, drinking and just lying around. They set off fireworks to celebrate New Year's, Chinese New Year's and the Fourth of July, and they cling to the cultural tradition of burning firecrackers to scare off evil spirits.

As a toddler in the early '60s, you would go with your folks to the brand-new Ala Moana Center or to Waikīkī, where you would visit the Honolulu Zoo or the Aquarium in the shadow of Diamond Head, or to Hanauma Bay, where you would hold out bits of bread or frozen peas and colorful tropical fish would try to nibble your baby toes. You could go barefoot anytime and just about anywhere because there was no ice or snow, no poison ivy and no snakes. Kids could go to public school barefoot unless there was to be a field trip. At the mall a sign on the escalator advises barefoot customers to take the elevator instead. Unofficially, the Hawai'i state footwear is the *slippah* or *zori* (never called flip-flops or thongs locally). Footwear, including *slippah* and closed shoes, are piled up outside the door and never worn in the house.

At drive in-style restaurants, you can get *saimin*, a noodle soup with exotic ingredients like roast pork and fish cake; or *kalua* pig, a dish of stringy bits of roast pork with a delightful smoky taste; and there is Hawai'i's version of *musubi*: a fist-sized block of rice topped with a slice of SPAM and wrapped in *nori* seaweed. Hawai'i takes the cake for consuming more SPAM per capita than any other state. It is common for drive-ins, lunch wagons and mom-and-pop restaurants to serve a "plate lunch" consisting of a fish, poultry or meat entrée or Hawaiian food dish, served with two scoops of rice, macaroni salad and, as if rice and macaroni weren't enough, a "choice of starch." The meal called *loco-moco* is a multi-cholesterol conglomeration of hamburger patty topped with gravy and a fried egg served over a mountain of white rice.

Where there's smoke there's fire, except sometimes in Hawai'i where billows of fragrant blue-gray smoke emanating from a schoolyard on the weekend mean that oil-soaked chickens are being roasted in a process called *huli-huli*, or turn-turn, so that some group can turn a profit. Kids raise money for their sports teams by selling Portuguese sweetbread, Portuguese sausage and chili from the popular Zippy's chain of local-style restaurants, named after the ZIP code. Some notable snacks that kids crave, from cradle to college dormitory, are dried plum-flavored *li hing mui*; salty and sweet crack seed; crunchy cracker-like treats called *senbei* and *kaki mochi*; the Chinese steamed bun *manapua*; boiled peanuts, salty and wet in the shell; and the deep-fried Portuguese doughnut called the *malasada*. Of all the rides, activities and *'ono*, or delicious, things to eat available at the annual Punahou Carnival, the longest lines, no matter how hard it rains, are for *malasadas*.

For Barry, the best treat was shave-ice, a cone of finely shaved ice topped with a rainbow of fruit-flavored syrups that instilled the sweetness of pineapple, passion fruit, mango or lychee into the snowball of ice. Some shave-ice shops would put vanilla ice cream in the bottom of the cone, and some even added soft sugar-soaked *azuki* beans.

Barry did a lot of things that other little boys his age did in Hawai'i and still do today: playing in the surf, learning to eat exotic foods, spending time with his *tūtū*, Grandmother Toot. As a small child, he did not know there was something unusual about being half-black and half-white. Or that there was anything unusual about growing up as the son of college students, who were themselves living on a meager student stipends subsidized by middle-class parents. Barry could not have imagined that it was at all unusual for a boy who looked like an African-American to be part of a family that consisted of a black man, a white woman and two white grandparents.

His young mother dropped out of school after completing less than a year of study. Though a new husband and new father, Barack Senior was a model student who never lightened his academic responsibilities. Instead he tackled an enormous course load, focusing on the methodology of econometrics—a combination of economic theory and mathematics. His long hours of study, away from his young wife and baby, brought outstanding academic results, and he graduated in just three years *summa cum laude* at the top of his class.

After his years at UH, Barack Senior was less skinny and more *akamai*, or wise, about the ways of the world, as he had seen it. In what would be an exit interview with newspaperman John Griffin, the Pollyanna view of Hawai'i that he had shared when he arrived had been modified. Now he saw Hawai'i with far more nuanced and realistic eyes. "Various races get along better here than on the Mainland or in parts of Africa," Obama said. But he added, "Hawai'i is not really a 'melting pot.'" Rather, Obama said, he sensed it was various races largely sticking with their own but co-existing peacefully, for the most part, with others.

It is typical for outsiders to think of Hawai'i as the classic "melting pot," the place where people of many races and backgrounds become one. That may have worked in Mainland cities, where Irish, Italian and Eastern European immigrants could gradually blend into the mainstream society over a generation or two. It was less true in Hawai'i, where by choice or necessity, the various ethnicities held on to their own cultures—and in some cases, even their own languages. Cooperation was possible and even necessary on the plantations as workers organized against the owners and bosses. But individual ethnic identities remained and flourished. Hawai'i, people came to say, was more like a good stew: It created a new whole, but the individual components remained instantly identifiable. It was no melting pot.

Obama told Griffin he personally had had little trouble. People were open to him and interested in his exotic story. But, Obama said, he did observe racial discrimination among the groups. It was, he mused, "rather strange… even rather amusing, to see Caucasians discriminated against here."

In early 1962, the New School for Social Research had offered Barack Senior a generous grant that would have enabled him to move his new family to New York City. However, when Harvard University offered a tuition-only grant, he chose to pursue the more prestigious path to a doctorate. The decision to go off to Harvard and leave Ann and Barry behind was a bombshell.

The much-talked-about marriage had lasted less than two years and did not create the beautiful music Ann had anticipated. By the summer, Barack Senior was in Harvard Yard, having abandoned his young wife and child for the promise of a PhD. from a prestigious U.S. university and thus a brighter future as an economist in Kenya. It seemed that Barack Senior had ambitions that could not be contained in tiny Hawai'i. After graduate studies at Harvard, he would go back to Kenya for a career that never quite matched the promise he showed during those early years at the University of Hawai'i.

When Barack Senior left Hawai'i, Ann, who had just turned 21, began to isolate herself from other students. She even moved away from Hawai'i briefly, to try life as a single mother and undergraduate at the University of Washington in Seattle. Sometime later she returned to Honolulu, and about this time she got a divorce. She resumed her multicultural lifestyle centered around the intellectual, international atmosphere of the East-West Center. A "mini United Nations" of students would gather regularly at the center's serene Japanese garden or meet for cheap meals at the center's Jefferson Hall cafeteria. In 1995, shortly after her death, the family held a remembrance service for Ann in that Japanese garden, a peaceful moment among the carefully tended trees and quiet stream that had been so special to her as a student.

As a child and even up to his 10th birthday, Barry did not have any clear memory of his father. By age six, he had seen only a few photos of his mom with his dad. What he knew about his father was based on some oft-repeated stories his mom and grandparents had told him. Although Gramps and Toot had come to embrace the African student as a son-in-law, they could not have been big fans after he picked up and moved clear across the country to Massachusetts.

Growing up, Barry was never certain how much to believe about his missing father. Had his father really been a goatherder back in Africa before he went to school? Was his father the son of a medicine man? Was it true that his father was a terrible driver and often wound up on the wrong side of the road because in Kenya they drive, as the British do, on the left side of the road? Had he actually dangled a friend by his heels over the steep cliff of the Nu'uanu Pali Lookout because the friend had dropped his favorite smoking pipe over the cliff? Had he shown up for an important university event wearing jeans and a leopard-print shirt while everyone wore suits and ties? Had he followed one of the most popular Hawaiian music acts at the university's

International Fair by standing up to sing some African songs, even though he was not a good singer?

Perhaps the story that influenced Barry the most was the one in which his father was said to have gone to a local bar where he was confronted by a man who said he would not drink in the same place with a "nigger." Rather than accept the insult with anger, his father had reportedly responded with an impromptu lecture on dignity and the rights of all men. According to the story, the man who had slung the insult pulled a hundred-dollar bill out of his wallet and offered it to Barry's father in an on-the-spot act of apology and penance. However unlikely that story seemed, it was confirmed in later years by another Hawai'i man who told candidate Obama that he had been there and witnessed the $100 act of contrition.

Even at the time of his father's death in 1982, Barack Obama would write, "My father remained a myth to me."

Barack Senior left Hawai'i in 1963. A year later, when Kenya was achieving independence from Britain, Ann was developing an interest in another exotic country that straddles the Equator: Indonesia. She had met another foreign student on the tennis court. Neither black nor white, Lolo Soetoro was Indonesian. Barry, who would grow to over 6 feet tall, remembered his stepdad Lolo was short and handsome, with smooth brown skin and thick black hair.

When Ann introduced her new beau to her father, Stanley Senior had a good laugh at the Indonesian's name. The word *lōlō* in the Hawaiian language means "paralyzed," "numb" "feeble-minded," though in the Islands' pidgin it simply means "crazy." And nearly everyone associates it with *pakalōlō*, the word for marijuana.

From the time Barry turned four till he reached age 10, Lolo was a father figure. Barack Obama recalled that Lolo was gentle and good-mannered, and as a boy, he admired the fact that Lolo was athletic and played a good game of tennis and enjoyed the arts of wrestling and boxing. Lolo also enjoyed playing chess and spent a lot of time at the Dunham home, challenging Gramps and putting up with his jokes. Barry said he sensed there was a special bond between Lolo and his mom, and at age six, boldly asked her if they were in love. As it turned out, they were in love, and Lolo had asked Ann to marry him. Things got complicated right away because Lolo, who had been sent to the East-West Center by the Indonesian government, was being called back to Jakarta. If Ann chose to marry him, she would have to move there. This time, Ann chose to go with her husband back to his homeland. ᙣ

CHAPTER FIVE

"A CHARGED AND CHALLENGING PLACE"
INDONESIA'S UNITY IN DIVERSITY

Barry was six years old when he moved to faraway Indonesia. He would spend four years there, and these formative years would shape his life and add depth to the boy he would be in Hawai'i and the man he would grow to be in Chicago and Washington. The experience would give him first-hand knowledge of how people around the world live in poverty under the yoke of dictatorship. He did not study this topic; he lived it.

Like Barry's biological father, his new stepdad, Lolo Soetoro, had been a foreign student in Hawai'i. Lolo was an amiable man. In Honolulu he was often mistaken for a Mexican. That mistake would never occur in Indonesia, where there were 107 million people with Lolo's ruddy brown skin, black hair and laughing black eyes.

A soil scientist, Lolo had been sent by the Indonesian government to further his study of geology under a grant from the East-West Center. In the midst of the 1967-68 school year, he was recalled, without warning, with other Indonesians studying abroad, to show their loyalty to a newly installed government. In March 1967, Indonesia's first president, Sukarno, had been deposed by one of his generals, another strongman named Suharto. The CIA was widely suspected of having engineered the bloody coup that replaced one dictator, who was supported by Communists, with another, who seemed more likely to align oil-rich Indonesia with the West. One wonders how well Washington knew its new Southeast Asian ally, but advisers probably knew there would be no kid gloves as Suharto struggled to gain control of the world's largest Muslim country.

Lolo had been witness to the uprising that had ousted the Dutch after they tried to reinstate themselves as colonial masters at the end of World War II. Lolo's father and brother, who had enlisted in the resistance movement, had been killed by the Dutch. Their house had been burned to the ground. Lolo was recalled in the wake of Suharto's reprisals against Sukarno's supporters. The rise to power of Indonesia's second president was a brutal episode in the country's history, and no one knows how many hundreds of thousands perished in an abortive Communist coup and the reprisals that followed. Upon his return to his homeland, Lolo was confronted with the dilemma that intellectuals in the Philippines later faced during the Ferdinand Marcos dictatorship: To what degree would he support President Suharto's New Order? Lolo was a practical man who understood power. He did what the new government asked of him. Conscripted into the Indonesian Army as a lieutenant, he traveled to New Guinea and later worked on military road-building and construction teams.

It would be a matter of months before Lolo's new American bride and stepson would be ready to travel abroad to join him. They would need to get their paperwork in order and endure shots against a variety of diseases such as smallpox and dysentery that were part of life in Indonesia. In the meantime, Gramps learned what he could about Indonesia and shared everything with them. Gramps associated Indonesia with the novelist Joseph Conrad's books about the Spice Islands. The most crowded island was Java, where nearly 70 percent of the population lived. That was where Mount Krakatoa blew up in August 1883 in one of the most violent volcanic explosions in recorded history. The largest and most primitive island was Borneo, where tribes kept shrunken heads of their enemies. Another was Sumatra, which straddles the Equator. "They have tigers and orangutans there, and headhunters, too," Gramps told the boy, although there were no tigers, orangutans or headhunters in Jakarta, the capital, where Barry would live.

In 1967, the year Suharto assumed the presidency, mother and son boarded a Pan Am jet in Honolulu and took off on their first great foreign adventure, which would be just that, the first of many adventures. On the way over, they stopped in Japan for three days. During their stay, they traveled an hour from Tokyo to see the magnificent Kamakura Daibutsu, a Buddha statue that stands more than 42 feet high.

Though Barry's mother had read about Indonesia and Gramps had told them so much about it, they were unaware of the Communist purge and reign of terror that had occurred less than two years earlier. Had she known of the violence and the continuing corruption on a massive scale, the peace-loving Ann Soetoro might not have made the trip. Nor could little Barry have been prepared for the dramatic change that would occur in his lifestyle. He was used to Honolulu's modern urban environment. If you ignore the palm trees and green mountains in the background, Honolulu is much like other American cities: There are paved streets with late-model cars and buses whizzing by, and the neighborhoods are laid out neatly and cleanly with cut lawns. Everything works in an orderly manner. That is not what is found in Indonesia. For the first-time visitor to Asia, Indonesia appears to be just the opposite of clean and orderly. In a word, chaotic.

Jakarta was a jumble of unplanned urban sprawl and villages masquerading as a Third World capital in the late '60s. After finding his wife and son at the airport, Lolo Soetoro had to negotiate their way through a throng of armed military men guarding the facility. Lolo had borrowed a car and drove through Indonesia's capital, a super-crowded, super-noisy collection of towns and villages sprawling across the densely populated tropical island of Java. Along their journey, the paved road gave way to a rough gravel road, which gave way to a rutted dirt road that ran along rice paddies until they came to a dirty brown river where villagers washed clothes and bathed. Men and women in the outlying areas wore only swaths of cloth called *sarong*. The little children wore only khaki shorts. They drove deeper into the rainforest until the car came to a stop.

Barry's new home was not in the city but in a *kampung*, or compound, of simple wooden and stucco houses topped with red roof tiles. The Soetoro house was a stone house, notable for the big mango tree that stood in the front courtyard. Work was still being done on Lolo's house to accommodate the newcomers from Hawai'i. That was the bad news. The good news was that Lolo's compound was like a private mini-zoo. Not only were there chickens, ducks and a big yellow dog, there were a plumed cockatoo and other exotic jungle birds, and two baby crocodiles. As if that weren't enough, Lolo said he had a real surprise for Barry. The boy heard it before he saw it: There was a howl from up in a tree. At the sight of a peanut in Lolo's hand, a long-haired, long-armed hairy animal scurried down the tree to grab the treat. "It's a monkey," said Barry. No, he was told, it was a hairy ape named Tata. Lolo had brought the dark-eyed, flat-headed ape all the way from New Guinea for Barry.

Now the six-year-old boy who had had neither a cat nor a dog nor even a canary in Hawai'i had an ape for a pet. Apart from exotic animals, life in the *kampung* was simple, more attuned to nature and more intertwined with the lives of neighbors, who in American terms lived in poverty. Barry's four years in Indonesia would teach him, better than any textbook could, the difference between a rich country and a poor one. Unlike Hawai'i-born kids his age, he would experience firsthand the difference between poverty and privilege. The Soetoro family might have been poor by American standards but not by Indonesian standards. There was always food. Their little family would eat their dinner of chicken curry on a small table under a single light bulb that hung from the rafters. Lolo taught Barry how to eat raw hot chili peppers, with plenty of rice.

Though trained as a geologist, Lolo was not paid well as an Army lieutenant. At the outset, the family had to get along without a refrigerator, an air conditioner or a TV set. Still, compared to other villagers, they were considered well off. Lolo could not afford to buy a car, but he would head off on a Japanese motorcycle to work on road projects. To help with family finances and to relieve her boredom, Barry's mom, now known as Ann Soetoro, found work teaching English to Indonesian businessmen at the American Embassy in the city. Ann learned as much as she taught from the Indonesians and Americans she met there. Much of what she heard from her circle of acquaintances about Indonesia's brutal brand of power politics and unceasing corruption clashed with the idyllic stories her husband had told before they came to Indonesia. He hadn't told them about the beggars and lepers they would encounter on a daily basis, like the man who came to their door with a hole where his nose should have been. Of the beggars, Obama the community organizer would later write: "They seemed to be everywhere, a gallery of ills—men, women, children, in tattered clothing matted with dirt, some without arms, others without feet, victims of scurvy or polio or leprosy." Mother and son became witnesses to the great divide between the privileged and the poor in Asia. In this challenging environment, Barry's mother proved to be someone who worked well with people of another culture and wanted to be among them. A humanist at heart, and a pragmatist at hand, she prepared Barry to be a man of the people, counseling him to be proud of who he was but not to look down on anyone else.

When school wasn't in session, Barry would play *futbal*, or what American kids call soccer. His friends called him "Berry," which sounded more mellifluous in the Malay-based Indonesian. One day when he was playing with the *kampung* kids an older kid from down the road snatched the ball away in the middle of the game. Barry took off after the older boy, who stopped running long enough to grab a rock and hurl it at Barry, hitting him in the head and drawing blood. When Lolo saw that Barry was bleeding, he was not amused. The next day, Lolo brought home boxing gloves. The boxing lessons began. Barry looked up to Lolo with fondness and respect and learned to defend himself. One of the lessons Lolo taught Barry was that strong men try to take advantage of weaker men and women. And countries are like men; strong countries will take advantage of weak countries. "It's better to be strong," he recalled. Barry did push-ups to build up his muscles. He did not have Wheaties, but Lolo, who believed that people take on the powers of the animals they eat, promised to bring him home some tiger meat. He was proud when his stepdad introduced him to Indonesians as his son, but the connection was more formal than familial, and there was no bond of blood between stepfather and stepson.

Before long Barry's mother became pregnant, and in 1970 she gave birth to a daughter, Maya. There is a picture of Barry with his mother and step-father and new baby sister sitting on a piece of hardwood furniture in their Jakarta home. Lolo is looking proud and casual in a white shirt and jeans. Barry's mom wears a traditional Indonesian outfit with a headscarf but short skirt. She holds Maya in what had to have been one of her first baby dresses. Barry looks quite content and well fed, if not a bit pudgy. His hair is short.

"My father really enjoyed having a boy around, teaching him things like boxing and chess," Maya would later say. "He wanted to adopt him. But Barack obviously felt the lack of his own father. My father couldn't offer everything Barack needed."

Like Hawai'i, Indonesia was a place of great diversity. From the 7th century to the 14th century, Hindu and Buddhist dynasties gathered and lost influence on the archipelago before Islam advanced and conquered. It was the Portuguese who sought and savored the tropical ingredients that branded these the Spice Islands. But it was the Dutch who worked for three centuries to stitch them together into a colony that could send raw materials and other riches back to Europe. Indonesia's thousands of islands stretch out to 576,000 square miles, an area the size of Texas. In modern times, an independent Republic of Indonesia, the world's fifth most populous nation, has held together, thanks in part to a national language, Bahasa Indonesia, and a national philosophy that reveres the center and draws the hundreds of ethnic groups and tribes to it.

When Indonesians fought their Dutch colonial masters and won independence, they inherited a nation that was at once the world's most populous Muslim country and also home to a Christian minority, a Hindu minority and scores of animist tribes. They wisely recognized that a nation of so many diverse cultures could only survive if each was tolerant of the other. Among the nation's five founding principles (collectively called the Pancasila, or five beliefs) are belief in God, belief in civilized humanity, belief in the unity of Indonesia, belief in democracy and belief in justice for all. The national motto of the huge archipelago, emblazoned on its national coat of arms, is "Unity in Diversity." This idea of respecting, indeed demanding, diversity, is a survival ethic held closely by governments not just in Indonesia but throughout Southeast Asia. Leaders know only too well that cracks in the carefully molded multiethnic order, if allowed to widen, lead to social chaos.

After the family settled in, the young boy was enrolled at the Catholic Elementary School Franciscus Assisi, where he attended grades 1 through 3. School records describe a "Barry Soetoro," an Indonesian citizen born in Honolulu, whose religion is listed as Islam. In his book, Barack Obama recalls that he learned the national language Bahasa Indonesia within six months and fell in easily with the local kids. He recalls that, with a few exceptions, he mingled well with them, learning much about their culture and legends. Along the way, he also survived chicken pox and measles and avoided getting any more diseases. He slept comfortably under a mosquito net to reduce the risk of getting malaria.

On the sweeter side, he learned to enjoy Indonesia's bounty of extraordinary, little-known tropical fruits, including the fabulous rambutan, which looks like a rubbery, hairy red egg with a sweet lychee-like center. As he remembered it, he was a happy and typical Indonesian kid, eating delectable tropical fruits and catching insects. He took part in kite-dueling competitions, a game that kids across the Asian continent have played for centuries. As he tells it: "The children of farmers, servants and low-level bureaucrats had become my best friends, and together we ran the streets morning and night, hustling odd jobs, catching crickets, battling swift kites with razor-sharp strings—the loser watched his kite soar off with the wind, and knew that somewhere other children had formed a long wobbly train, their heads to the sky, waiting for their prize to fall from the sky."

Barry's former teachers and playmates in his old neighborhood of Betawi remembered "Berry" as a well-fed, chubby boy who wore Bermuda shorts. His first-grade teacher recalled that little Barry was having trouble with the Indonesian language and struggled with his lessons. Nevertheless, even as a child he was a natural leader, and the other kids would follow him. He would pick up the younger children when they fell, and he would tattle on the older kids when they broke the rules. One of his teachers laughed when Barry proclaimed in one of his first essays that he wanted to make people happy and be president. He did not say president of what.

Neighborhood kids and schoolmates teased him mercilessly because he was blacker than they were and because he never learned to speak their language well. Now in their mid-40s, his former schoolmates remembered calling him "Negro," throwing rocks at him and on one occasion, tying his hands and feet and throwing him in a swamp, and then holding his head under the surface of the murky water. The underwater mini-torture was reserved for Barry because they knew the Hawai'i kid could swim. Those who remember getting into fights with him say he was hard to beat because he was heavier than they were. It took two or three of them to take him down. Another classmate remembered they made fun of Barry by wrapping a sarong on him Muslim style "even though he didn't pray." On another occasion they told him that a chunk of anchovylike shrimp paste was chocolate. By this time, he had learned the word *"curang,"* which means "cheat," and had many occasions to use it. Some of his friends were mystified that he had been allowed by his parents to be left-handed, because in Indonesia left-handed children are broken of that habit and forced to learn to write with their right hand.

Barry might have been bullied and called names, but many of his experiences were good. Years later he would describe with fond memories the fun he had playing with Tata, his pet ape, and how thrilled he was to learn about Hanuman, Indonesia's much-loved monkey god deity. He recalls with a wry smile some of the unusual snacks he ate as a boy: Dog meat was tough but snake meat was tougher. Grilled grasshopper was considered a crunchy treat. Still, not everything he did as a boy in Jakarta was unusual. He joined an Indonesian Boy Scout troop and learned how to Be Prepared in Indonesia. He swam a lot and played with turtles.

When Barry was in the fourth grade, his parents moved to Menteng, the leafy, elite neighborhood in central Jakarta where many expatriate business executives, foreign diplomats and high-ranking Indonesian officials like Suharto lived. He attended Government Elementary School Menteng 1, which was also called the Besuki Public School. The school was built by the Dutch colonial government in the 1930s and was well known after World War II as the local school for the children of expatriate and Indonesian businessmen. In the '60s it was taken over by a Muslim foundation, but Barry Soetoro did not receive a traditional Muslim education. Despite some unfounded and highly sensational news reports that circulated during the primary campaign about its being a radical Islamic *madrassa*, or school for terrorists, Menteng 1 was a mixed non-religious school where Barry studied alongside Muslims, Protestants, Catholics, Hindus, Buddhists and Confucians in the spirit of the Pancasila.

In his time, Barry was required to study passages from the Koran, and one of his teachers pointed out to his mother that the boy made faces during Muslim religion lessons. Barry's mother was not overly concerned, he recalled. "'Be respectful,' she'd say," he wrote in his autobiography. His elementary school classmates remember that he sat in the back of the class. They recalled watching his left hand in amazement as he sketched American cartoon heroes. His claim to fame was how well he could sketch Batman and Spiderman.

In 2007 and 2008, journalists from all over the world visited Jarkarta to see where Barack Obama had lived. The American TV show *Inside Edition* sent a crew to visit both schools he had attended. At the Assisi Catholic Grammar School, the reporter and cameraman were greeted by little boys in shorts and little girls in plaid skirts, all wearing clean white shirts. Inside, the reporter found those school records that listed Islam as his faith because his father was a Muslim. The TV show clarified that Senator Obama himself was never a Muslim and is in fact a devout Christian. An Assisi teacher recalled, "He was good in mathematics."

Across the smog-filled city, the crew visited the Besuki public school, which is built around a central recreation yard emblazoned with logos from the chocolate drink Milo. There hundreds of happy-looking children wore school uniforms composed of white shorts and batik shirts, while some female students in a student body that is now 90 percent Muslim also wore white headscarves. A former student of the school pointed out the wooden bench where he had sat next to Barry Soetoro. Every day at noon, the Muslim children were called to prayer, while six Christian children sat in a small chapel where they sang and read the Bible. When a writer from the *New York Times* visited Besuki School several months earlier, he saw a sign that proclaimed in Bahasa, "I understand that we are all different and include everyone."

While Barry was a student in Indonesian schools, taught in the Indonesian language, his mother saw to it that he also got an American education, reading and writing in English. She signed up for a U.S. correspondence course and woke him up every morning at 4 a.m. to home teach him the American courses in English. They pored over the correspondence course lessons for three hours each morning, five days a week, before she went to work at the American Embassy. There she continued teaching English to Indonesian businessmen. Workers at the Embassy's U.S. Information Service Library remember that Barry would sometimes hang out in the library, amusing himself with comic books and American magazines and doing his American homework while his mother spent time with her adult students.

From time to time, Ann would take her son to the American Club, where his carefree days of play with his Indonesian pals would be balanced by time around the pool, sipping Coca-Colas and watching American cartoons.

When Barry's Indonesian classmates started the fifth grade at Menteng School, they found that Barry was not among them. He was headed for Hawai'i, where he would live with his grandparents again and eat all the ice cream he wanted. His mother said she and baby Maya would come to visit at Christmas and move back to Hawai'i within a year or so. And so Barry left for Honolulu in the summer of 1971. Nearly 10 years after his biological father had left him, he was being parted from another parent.

Barry might have guessed that his mom's marriage to his stepfather was on rocky ground. Ann was becoming disillusioned with Lolo's dismissals of the way things were in Indonesia. He would offer excuses for the power politics and corruption that cloaked the country and clogged the wheels of everything it tried to accomplish. In reaction to this, she told Barry to treasure the hardheaded convictions about doing the right thing and fighting the system that had been the hallmarks of his biological father. That was his inheritance, she told him. Having watched the civil rights movement unfold and take hold in the United States from outposts in Honolulu and Jakarta, Ann Soetoro had developed a strong feeling for the struggle for equality being waged by African-Americans and Freedom Riders and their supporters. The politician Barack Obama would later observe that much of what he had learned about America's tumultuous politics and social movements of the '60s came to him filtered by his mother's incorruptible idealism and liberalism.

Her thinking was strongly influenced by the speeches of Dr. Martin Luther King, Jr., who in 1967 was finally recognized with the Nobel Peace Prize. Her tastes in music tended toward folk songs with a political message. She loved the music of the African folk singer Miriam Makeba and the looks of Caribbean-style singing star Harry Belafonte, whom she called "the most handsome man on Earth." Somehow the white-skinned girl was developing something of a black soul. She wore loose, flowing colorful clothes, a fashion that would become associated with the San Francisco's hippie movement in the late '60s. The Indonesians she befriended said she seemed to have a deep, abiding love for the downtrodden people of the world. "You know," said one of her friends, "Ann was really, really white, but she just loved people of a different skin color—brown people."

Apart from her part-time job at the Embassy, Ann began to spend time with artisans who were keeping Indonesian arts and crafts alive. She had studied weaving in college and maintained an interest in making things by hand. As she was delving into Indonesia's traditional culture, Lolo was moving up modern Indonesia's ladder of success. Indonesia is a major oil exporter, and in the '70s the oil business was booming there as it had in Kansas 50 years earlier. Thanks in part to his experience living abroad as an East-West Center grantee and in part to a brother-in-law who worked in Jakarta for California's Union Oil Company, Lolo was hired by Union's Government Affairs Office. The high-paying job in the capital made it possible for Lolo to buy a car and a TV and mix socially with expatriate businesspeople in Jakarta and up-and-coming Indonesians who spoke English. He became obsessively fond of Andy Williams' recording of "Moon River" and Johnnie Walker Black Label scotch. Ironically, Lolo Soetoro was becoming more Westernized at the same time that Ann Soetoro was becoming more Easternized. Terrance Bigalke, director of the Education Program at the East-West Center, worked with Ann at the Ford Foundation in Jakarta years later, long after she had separated from Lolo. Her differences with Lolo were not so much the divide between East and West, although that was part of it; rather, it was more a matter of social class, Bigalke said. "Lolo wanted to move into the upper middle-class community. Ann's interest was in staying with the poor," Bigalke said.

Barack Obama said his mother was prepared for the hardship of living as the white wife of an Indonesian bureaucrat, but she was not prepared for the loneliness that weighed upon her. Her bold experiment of marrying an Indonesian in order to share with him the excitement of nation-building in Southeast Asia had lost its allure. They separated, and Ann returned to Hawai'i to live with Barry and the new baby sister born in Indonesia. Barry would live in Hawai'i longer than his mother, and he would return to Indonesia several times to visit, but he would not live overseas again. Ann's globetrotting lifestyle, though, had just begun. Once she completed her advanced studies in anthropology at the University of Hawai'i, she would return to Indonesia as a researcher, and wind up spending many years working with traditional weavers and ironworkers and craftswomen in rural parts of Asia, helping them find money to invest in materials and markets to sell their products.

Ann was more than willing to buck authority and traditional thinking. Her work with small craftsmen demonstrated that. The government was trying to force peddlers and tradesmen off the street and into contained centers where they could be managed and taxed. Ann felt this was killing entrepreneurial energy. "To work in that sector at that point was a bit risky," Bigalke said. "It took courage to work in that sector when the government was trying to get people off the street." As she went about her work, independent-minded Ann Soetoro cut an imposing figure. By then she had put on considerable weight and was known to dress in her own style, with flowing *batik* skirts, Indonesian fabrics, hoop earrings and colorful jewelry. "She wasn't a retiring person at all," Bigalke said. "She was sure of herself and knew what she was doing was right. I really respect Ann for standing her ground on things that she felt important." Those things included battling to provide support and encouragement for small businesses and community artisans at a time the focus of development assistance was on big money, big projects. In some ways, Barack Obama followed this pattern set down by his mother, when he chose community development over the lure of a big-money law firm. "That makes a strong statement," Bigalke said. "They worked in the same segment of society, but in different cultures."

Twenty-five years after leaving Indonesia, the adult Barack Obama recalled the Southeast Asian nation he lived in as "a charged and challenging place" where "my vision had been permanently altered." Obama said his life in Indonesia had opened his eyes to extremes of poverty and wealth and the far-reaching impact political upheaval can have on ordinary people. "It gave me an enormous appreciation for the magnificent culture and history of Asia," he told reporters. "It gave me a great love for the people of Asia. It made me mindful of the huge gaps in opportunity that exist in many countries of the world. It also made me appreciate how deeply impoverished people can be—how issues of corruption can thwart opportunity." ∞

CHAPTER SIX

"Wrestling with a ghost"
Barry Meets His Father

Back in Honolulu, Barry's refuge from his fifth-grade demons was the 10th-floor apartment where he lived with his mother's parents, Stanley and Madelyn Dunham, or Gramps and Toot. Toot was short for *tūtū*, the Hawaiian word for a grandparent, especially a grandmother. In Hawai'i, kids of all ethnic backgrounds talk about their *tūtū*. Madelyn Dunham, who was ambitiously pursuing her career as a bank executive, did not want to think of herself as a grandmother. She preferred to be called Toot by Barry, so Toot it was. The Dunhams were mildly liberal humanists, but conservative in politics. They abhorred racial discrimination and the way loyal Japanese-American citizens had been interned in World War II, but they voted for Richard M. Nixon in 1968.

In the '70s, when Barry lived with them, the Dunhams were in their 50s. Gramps was tall, lanky and gray-haired, as he had been much of his life. He almost always wore eyeglasses. After arriving in Hawai'i, he had abandoned dark suits for the bright floral print shirts called aloha shirts. Gramps had come to Honolulu to manage a furniture store. He had worked on oil rigs, served in the Army and dreamed of being a poet. Nonetheless he found his calling as a salesman. It was his job to earn the confidence of people from all walks of life who came to look at furniture. The best-selling advice book *How to Make Friends and Influence People* by Dale Carnegie had shaped him to become a positive-thinking person who expected the most from every exchange. Gramps took this advice to heart and melded it with what he knew of the traditional Aloha Spirit of welcoming and caring for strangers. With this open, positive outlook, he became an outwardly friendly guy who accepted everyone at face value.

Even when he was living in Indonesia, Barry spent had summers with Gramps and Toot. When the first men to walk on the moon arrived in Hawai'i days after their July 20, 1969, splashdown in the Pacific, Gramps and Barry were among the thousands who turned out to greet them when they were brought ashore at Hickam Air Force Base. Barry remembered that Gramps hoisted him on his shoulders so he could glimpse the Apollo 11 moon men as they waved to the crowd from their isolation van. Years later Obama would recount that incident to illustrate his proud all-American patriotic outlook and upbringing.

Barry had fond memories of going with Gramps to 'A'ala Park and Waikīkī to play checkers with Filipino men, who smoked cigars or chewed a type of betel nut that stained their teeth red. A Portuguese man who had bought a sofa from Gramps took them spearfishing on O'ahu's Windward side. The generous Hawaiians that Gramps worked with sometimes invited him and Toot and Little Barry to family feasts called *lū'au*, where the excitement was about *kalua*, a whole pig roasted by hot stones in the earth, and *poi*, the pudding-like staple made from the taro root. Gramps would dig in, but Toot politely declined to partake in these local delicacies. Still, when guests came to the apartment, the Dunhams always served *sashimi*, delicately sliced strips of raw red fish called *'ahi*, which most Americans eat after it's cooked and packed in tins labeled "tuna." Gramps also brought Barry to bridge games and poker parties with some black men he knew.

In his memoir, Barack Obama recalled that one of Gramps' black friends was an old man with a graying Afro who boasted of his days in Chicago when the celebrated writers Langston Hughes and Richard Wright were making their names. Frank Marshall Davis was a published poet and shared his verses with Gramps, who likewise had leanings toward poetry. Frank liked to point out that both he and Gramps came originally from Kansas, although from different sides of the tracks. Though Gramps and his friend shared whiskey from a jam jar and wrangled limericks together, Barry sensed that their life experiences were so different as to form an invisible barrier between them. Years later, Barry would learn that Davis had lived in Wichita at a time when a black man had to move off the sidewalk if a white man was coming. Davis doubted that his latter-day friend Stan Dunham or any white man could understand what it was like to be routinely and regularly humiliated by racial discrimination, although he eventually told Barry he thought a Native Hawaiian might well understand. In time Davis would share many lessons with the young high school student, lessons both painful and profound.

Gramps loved to tell jokes he picked up from the *Reader's Digest* and stories of questionable taste. He was a whiz at coming up with one-liners and statements that stretched the truth from here to eternity. Once when tourists were taking a picture of little Barry playing in the sand, Gramps came up behind them and solemnly informed them that the boy was actually the son of King Kamehameha I. Besides the fact that Barry's father came from Africa, Kamehameha the Great died in 1819. While Gramps was a kidder, Toot was more pragmatic and didn't voice her opinion very often. She usually let Gramps get away with whatever he was saying. She pleased Barry by making that all-American favorite dessert, Jell-O.

Now that Barry was 10, he sensed a change in Gramps, who had switched jobs, moving from his life's work of selling furniture to the more promising arena of life-insurance sales. But he wasn't successful in the new career, and after failing to sign customers or being rebuked by bosses, he was often morose. That can-do determination he had developed in the Great Depression and nurtured through World War II and the Cold War was disappearing as fast as the nation was changing. The likeable guy Barry had seen as a youngster had disappeared too. Barry could see the disappointment on Gramps' face, and he saw too that Gramps was becoming a grouch.

While Gramps was on the decline, Toot was on the rise. She had joined the Bank of Hawaii in 1960, and by 1970, Madelyn Dunham had become one of the first two women to be named a vice president of Hawai'i's premier bank in terms of assets. She would leave the apartment every morning promptly at 6:30 to catch the bus, looking businesslike in a tailored woman's suit and high heels. At the bank, she was known as a tough boss who was feared by junior employees because she demanded high standards of performance from them, with no tolerance for slacking off or doing things Island-style. But those who worked with Madelyn also remember her soft side and willingness to mentor the young men who would have her as a boss.

At home, she was by and large the obliging wife. Sometimes Gramps and Toot would argue over silly things, like how to cook a steak. Barry came to think that Gramps was jealous that Toot earned more money than he did. For all his jealousy and disappointment, Gramps was still a dreamer filled with poems and sketches and plans for the future. Through it all, Barry's grandparents loved him unconditionally, but there was no doubt in anyone's mind that he was a boy who missed his mother, and a boy who had no real memory of being with his father.

Sometimes after school, Barry would go to the library. Most of the time he would go straight home. On occasion his Punahou classmates would accompany him to the little apartment to "just hang out." Often Gramps would open the door for Barry and then take a nap. This gave Barry time to read comic books or watch sitcoms on TV. In the days before communications satellites were positioned over the Pacific Ocean, viewers in Hawai'i would see network television shows a week later than other Americans because the tapes of weekly shows were flown to Hawai'i for rebroadcast in the same time slot, seven days later. It wasn't until November 1966 that the pioneering communications satellite called Lani Bird made it possible for Islanders to watch "live" sporting events in what is now called real time. Barry was a beneficiary of the new technology and watched live the same TV shows that other American kids were watching.

Young as he was, Barry picked up on the fact that most people on television didn't look like him. If there were black actors on TV, they were typically butlers or servants or sidekicks. Barry was happy to discover the show *I Spy*, co-starring Bill Cosby, the first black man to have a starring role in a prime-time American TV series. What was more, Cosby played a cool guy who was hip and well dressed, athletic and brainy, a Rhodes Scholar who was up to every challenge his career in espionage threw at him. Living in Hawai'i, surrounded by Asian-Americans, Barry was also aware that Asians were seldom portrayed in a positive light or in situations that resembled the real world.

Sometimes he and Gramps would eat TV dinners on individual folding tray tables set up in front of their chairs. After dinner, Gramps would sit in a big extra-stuffed armchair and sip a drink or improvise a way to clean his teeth with a bit of the cellophane wrapper he would pull off his pack of cigarettes. The start of the *Tonight Show* with Johnny Carson at 10:00 was the signal for Barry to go to his room. There he would lie in bed, listen to a Top 40 radio station, and reflect on his experiences at Punahou School and the streets of Honolulu.

It was just before Christmas 1971, a few months after Barry Obama started Punahou, that he had his first conversation with his father, during what would be the only time they spent together face-to-face.

Barry's father had written ahead to tell the Dunhams that he would be coming from Kenya for a visit around Christmas. Barack Senior was recuperating from a car accident and wanted to take some time off from his demanding work as a senior economist in the Ministry of Finance in Nairobi. Barry's mom and baby sister Maya were also planning to visit from Jakarta at Christmas. All of them—Gramps and Toot, Barry, his mom and his baby sister—would be together for the first time, along with the absent Obama, who had left them 10 years earlier. It is hard to imagine who among them was the most stressed by the visit. Barry would finally find out if the man lived up to the myth. His mom would discover what it was like to be with her ex-husband for the first time in years. His half-sister would be meeting her first African. Gramps and Toot would be facing the man who had abandoned their daughter and her first-born child to forge his own life in Kenya. Barry was not looking forward to meeting his father. Just as he was becoming accustomed to thinking of himself as a Hawai'i kid, he was going to be immersed in his largely unexplored and unwelcome Africanness.

For eight years, Barry had heard the often-repeated apocryphal stories about his brilliant, debonair father who could easily win people over. He trembled at the thought of meeting him in the flesh. Finally came the day of his father's arrival. Knowing his father was on his way to the apartment from the airport, Barry dragged himself home. On the way, he must have recalled the often-told tales he'd heard about what his father had said and done as a university student a decade earlier. Would the man be every bit the princely African man he had heard so much about? Would he be friendlier than his pictures suggested, or even more formal? Did he know anything about kids?

Then, as if he were a guest making an appearance on the *Johnny Carson Show*, there he was. Barack Obama Senior came toward him. At first he looked resplendent in his blue blazer, crisp white shirt and red scarf, every bit the high-ranking African government official. But when the man moved closer and into the light, Barry noticed that he was thinner than he had imagined. Perhaps he had lost a lot of weight. And the man walked with a limp and carried an ivory-handled cane. He seemed fragile. And behind his horn-rimmed glasses, his eyes looked yellow as if he had a tropical disease, yellow fever or malaria.

He looked Barry over without saying much, and then remembered he had brought souvenirs for his son. He held out three miniature wooden carvings from Africa: an elephant, a lion and a man in tribal attire beating a drum. Barry thanked him stiffly. Because they could not all stay in the little apartment, the Dunhams had arranged for Barry's dad to stay in another apartment, and following the presentation of gifts, he adjourned with his suitcases to get settled. It was understood that they would gather every night in the Dunhams' living room, as if they were a real family.

Somehow Barry did not feel his father was the African prince he had once boasted about. He would pay a price for that little lie a few days later, but for now he pondered the fresh idea that he actually had a flesh-and-blood father, and wondered if perhaps his father would stay on in Hawai'i. Had his father ever played soccer or basketball? It was a fairly sure thing that even though he had gone to Harvard University, he could not throw a football.

Over the next few days and weeks, the mixed family did tourist things and revisited the places where Barack Senior had lived and where Gramps and Toot had lived near the University of Hawai'i. Though they spent time together and talked, Barry would later remark that he couldn't remember any conversation he had had with his father over the course of the four-week stay. "There was so much to tell, so much explaining to do in that single month, yet when I reach back into my memory for the words of my father, the small interactions or conversations we might have had, they seem irretrievably lost."

Lost as well was Barry's nascent desire to have this strange man around permanently. He began to count the days, not until Santa Claus would come, but until his father would go. While he couldn't recall specific conversations, he did remember several incidents, including the time he wanted to watch the TV program ·The Grinch That Stole Christmas, and his mom said he could but his father forbade him to. Barry Senior said that if his son had finished his homework, he should begin on the next day's homework. And he said something like "You're not working hard enough." These were the authoritarian pronouncements of a man he hardly knew. He was hurt, but these incidents weren't nearly as embarrassing as what happened in school later that week.

His embarrassingly Afrocentric father actually came to his home-room class to give a speech about life in Kenya. In Barry's mind this was a travesty, but Mrs. Hefty had invited Obama Senior and, not only that, she had invited another class to join the audience. For starters, everyone in the school would know that Barry Obama was not the son of a prince. He was the son of a bureaucrat, although an exotic one. Hefty's teaching colleague Eldredge vividly remembers Barack Senior's appearance before the fifth graders. Formidable in sandals, an African wraparound skirt similar to the Samoan *lava lava* and an untucked shirt of bright orange, the senior Obama lectured the students on Africa and the importance of education. The students were impressed by the speaker and started thinking that they were privileged to be attending Punahou where students could get to meet a real live African. In fact, many of Barry's classmates remembered that day in homeroom class for the rest of their lives. They also recalled that Mrs. Hefty had told them time and again that anybody in their class could grow up to be president. Years later, when Obama was asked to name a teacher who had influenced him, he chose Mabel Hefty because, he said, she could make every fifth-grader "feel special."

A few other strong memories of his father's visit stayed with him.

His father took him to his first jazz concert, to hear a popular jazzman named Dave Brubeck.

His father gave him his first basketball. In a rare photo of the family together, they are standing in front of a Christmas tree and Barry is holding the ball he has been given, while his father wears the necktie he has received.

And on his last day in Hawai'i, his father remembered that he had brought two 45 RPM records from Kenya. The family listened as the first of the records began to spin on Gramps' stereo. A chorus of voices in a strange language rose to the strains of guitar and horns, against the drumming. "Listen," his father told him: "The sound of your continent." With that, his father launched spontaneously into a dance, an African version of the *hula*, telling his son, "Now you will learn from the master."

There is a photograph of Barry and his father standing together at Honolulu Airport, which has been decorated for Christmas. Barack Senior looks like a diplomat or a jazzman with close-cropped hair and black glasses. He wears a jacket and tie, and has Barry in a half-hug with one arm across the boy's chest. Barry is smiling broadly with his own arms across his chest. He was either proud to have a father in the flesh or maybe he was just good at posing for pictures. In the pictures taken of Barry as a boy in Hawai'i or Indonesia, he is always smiling.

Years later, Barry's mother would tell him that she had divorced Barack Senior and that the break-up was not entirely her husband's fault. A lot of it had to do with who she was. For one thing, there was no getting over Barry's Kenyan grandfather's objection to the marriage, and then there was the issue of Barack Senior's first wife, whom he had not divorced. Barack Senior was not bothered by the legalistic details of his polygamous marriages. When he came to visit Barry that Christmas in 1971, he had suggested that Ann and Barry come back to live with him in Nairobi. Indeed, the Obama clan had been waiting for them. Later as an adult, after his father's death, the student and politician Barack Obama would travel to Kenya twice to learn more about the man and match the stories he had heard as a child with the very different ones that were told in his father's homeland.

In a speech at the University of Nairobi, Kenya, Barack Obama told of his first trip there when he had gone to Alego to discover his African roots. For the first time, he said, he "began to understand and appreciate the distance his father had traveled—from being a boy herding goats, to a student at the University of Hawai'i and Harvard University, to the respected economist that he was upon his return to Kenya."

In many ways, his father had embodied the New Africa of the early '60s, he said. He had returned to Kenya with the training he had received in Hawai'i and Harvard, hoping to help build a new nation.

As a boy in Hawai'i, Barry had grown up thinking of his father as a vibrant man who was a brilliant scholar, a generous friend and a leader of his country. Though his first trip to Kenya was "magical," it took the shine off his father's myth. "I discovered that for all his education, my father's life ended up being filled with disappointments. His ideas about how Kenya should progress often put him at odds with the politics of tribe and patronage, and because he spoke his mind, sometimes to a fault, he ended up being fired from his job and prevented from finding work in the country for many, many years. And on a more personal level, because he never fully reconciled the traditions of his village with more modern conceptions of family—because he related to women as his father had, expecting them to obey him no matter what he did—his family life was unstable, and his children never knew him well."

As an adult, Barry would learn that Barack Obama Senior had fathered eight children with four women, two white women and two African women. By all accounts he did not treat any of them very well for very long. After measuring his father's accomplishments against myths that had loomed so large, Barack Obama concluded in his memoir, "All my life, I had been wrestling with nothing more than a ghost!" Yet in a Father's Day speech on the campaign trail in South Carolina, candidate Obama would say he thinks of his own father every year around that day. ∞

CHAPTER SEVEN

"TRAPPED BETWEEN TWO WORLDS"
CHOOSING BETWEEN BLACK AND WHITE

In the months and years after his yuletide meeting with his father, Barry wrestled with the two ethnicities that were part of him. On the one side, his father's exotic, all-defining Africanness was a distinguishing, inescapable part of him. On the other side was his mother's *haole*-ness backed by his grandparents' middle-of-the-American-road lifestyle, which he shared.

When Ann Soetoro separated from her Indonesian second husband, she returned to Honolulu. This time she was on an East-West Center grant to study anthropology at the University of Hawai'i and take part in the center's Culture Learning Institute. Barry moved in with his mother and sister, happy to be away from the old folks at Gramps's place. Now maybe he could stay up after Johnny Carson came on. For three years, while he was in middle school, he would live with his mother and half-sister Maya in a small apartment on Poki Street. The apartment, though cramped, was well situated, a long field goal kick from Punahou School and a six- or seven-minute walk back to Gramps and Toot's place.

Maya Soetoro-Ng remembered her time on Poki Street as a happy time, spent together with her mother and brother. It was to be the only time the three lived together as a family, although they remained spiritually close and looked forward to reunions on special occasions. Maya's earliest memories of Honolulu are of a big chair in the Poki Street apartment and how she and her older brother would rock in it until it fell over backward, causing great laughter. She was three and he was 12. They grew up like most kids, with television and toys and the usual big-brother/baby-sister rivalry and harmony. About to enter his teens in the age of the Jackson Five, Barry was wearing his hair in the Afro style. Soetoro-Ng recalled that Barry was a cool cat who didn't take himself seriously. "He let me mess with his 'fro," she said. Anyway, he could fix his hair anytime because, Maya recalled, Barry always had an Afro pick comb in his back pocket.

"Our childhood was interesting," Soetoro-Ng would later muse. "It was broad. Our lives involved a lot of drifting in and out of worlds here and there. I think we were a little untethered."

If these were happy years for the Obama/Soetoros, they were also lean years for Barry. He was a shy kid trying to be popular, or at least not unpopular, with his schoolmates. Being raised by a single mother who was living on a graduate-student stipend meant not having a lot of expensive things. This was in stark contrast to many of his schoolmates who wanted for nothing, whose parents were among Honolulu's rich and famous. As a boy growing up in small apartments, Barry was envious of his classmates' split-level houses with big backyards and swimming pools.

With neither husband's support, it was difficult for Barry's mother to raise him and his sister on one salary, he said, and they struggled financially to get through each month. This was the period when his mother was accepting food stamps to supplement her budget. Some of his friends had stay-at-home moms, a few might even have had servants, but Barry did not. He was embarrassed when friends came over because the Poki Street apartment didn't have a big refrigerator and, worse yet, there wasn't much in the small fridge to share with kids who were on the prowl for after-school snacks. When he groused about it or the generally messy condition of the apartment, his mother set him straight, reminding him that she was a single mom with two kids and a heavy academic load and did not have time to bake cookies. She did not see herself as Mrs. Cleaver in *Leave It to Beaver*.

Barry tried his best to help his mom when he could, assisting with household chores, shopping and laundry. As a teen, he worked part time, especially in the summer. One of his first jobs was at the Baskin-Robbins ice cream store on South King Street just around the corner from Gramps' apartment. While some of his classmates were born with silver spoons, Barry gained workaday experience handing out pink plastic spoons with the 31 flavors he scooped. Wearing the shop's very uncool brown smock and cap gave him perspective.

"I'm sure that helped shape some of my attitudes as well, just in the sense of sort of an appreciation of people who are having to work hard to get where they need to go, because nothing would be handed to them. I think it made me hungrier, a little hungrier than I might have otherwise been," he later told *U.S. News and World Report*. Hungry, but not for ice cream. Though he would incorporate a visit to Baskin-Robbins into his dating ritual, right up to the time he married, he didn't care much for ice cream after all that scooping in his teen years.

Older brother Barry also helped baby-sit Maya, whom he later described as "the knowing, dark-eyed child that my sister had become." Soetoro-Ng, who became a close confidant in later years, never thought of her older brother as a brooding adolescent or teen. She saw him as an "intelligent, sensitive, thoughtful, fun-loving" young man who had plenty of friends but who was also bookish and sometimes wrapped up in solitude.

"He was always restless," his sister told a *New York Times* reporter. "There was always somewhere else he needed to go."

Restless as he was, he could not wait for answers to come to him. He had to go looking for them. In retrospect, Maya said, her brother believed that his Punahou friends were pushing an identity on him, and that put pressure on him to put a name on himself.

Barry felt that people did not see him as an ordinary human being first and a black or half-black kid second. The first thing they saw was an African face leavened with Caucasian blood. His classmates maintain that being of two or more ethnic backgrounds carried no social stigma at Punahou. In fact, Barry's classmates say they considered someone who was half-Caucasian more intriguing than someone who was of a single ethnicity; and they considered someone who was a mixture of races, for example, Hawaiian-Chinese-Irish-Native American-Portuguese, to be more interesting, attractive and exotic than someone who was merely of two ethnicities.

But looking back on who he had been and how he had felt then, Barack Obama said he was trapped between two worlds. At 12 or 13, he was at a stage of development when he had to define himself, one way or another. He had to choose a race.

Sensitive and self-conscious Barry did not want to be seen as someone of mixed race. He did not want to be half a loaf of something. He chose to identify himself as black, choosing not, as he put it, "to advertise my mother's race." In *Dreams*, he said he took this course because he did not want to be a tragic mulatto figure and did not want to forever ingratiate himself to whites. He did not want others to look at his face, see the telltale signs of mixed race, and take his measure against their own evolving ideas of what it was to be *hapa*. Obama's classmates say they don't remember him as a person struggling to create an identity, let alone a black or African-American identity. But they did notice one remarkable change in their friend about that time: his gait. "The way he walked—his walk changed," said former teacher and coach Eldredge, who would see Obama around the Punahou campus. Barry had adopted an athletic, loping, shoulder-swinging gait. "Even his classmates mentioned it," Eldredge said, "his gait, how it changed."

Still, in his memoir, Obama wrote: "Privately, they guessed at my troubled heart, I suppose—the mixed blood, the divided soul, the ghostly image of the tragic mulatto trapped between two worlds."

On one level, Barry's choice seemed to resonate with Eleanor Roosevelt's remark that "No one can make you feel inferior without your consent." In that regard, young Barry Obama was resolute about not granting anyone the right to make him feel guilt or shame about being of mixed blood.

On the other hand, he was in Hawai'i, where about half of all births of permanent residents in the '70s involved more than one ethnicity. For reasons peculiar to Hawai'i's history, people described themselves as Hawaiian, Japanese, Chinese, Portuguese, Filipino, Korean, Samoan, Tongan, *haole* or white, *popolo* or black, or *hapa*, half, meaning of mixed race. No one group had a simple majority, and no one thought it unusual that someone's ethnicity might be a mixture of two, three, four or more of the above. In fact, it was and is considered a positive attribute, contributing to the fabled beauty of Island women and the popular image of the handsome Waikīkī beachboy.

Peter Apo, a Hawaiian statesman, entertainer and tourism adviser, noted that the high percentage of mixed-race marriages distinguishes Hawai'i from other places with multiethnic melting-pot populations. "While other cities like New York and Los Angeles also boast large percentages of multicultural populations—only in Hawai'i do we routinely marry each other. This cross-cultural tolerance and unconditional acceptance of strangers to the highest levels of personal intimacy is an inheritance from the Hawaiian host culture. This phenomenon of life in Hawai'i has produced an astounding array of *hapa*-children who are truly multicultural and who flow so easily between the lines."

Even more remarkable about Barry's decision to black out his white side and his *hapa* identity was that he was living with his mother, and white grandparents, who had themselves adjusted to living in an uncommonly multiracial, multiethnic community. Around the time he entered high school, he separated himself from Gramps, who had accompanied him on his earliest adventures in Hawai'i.

Ironically, it was his white mother who had provided Barry with positive reinforcement for the black ancestry that was bequeathed to him. Over the years, when they lived together in Indonesia and Hawai'i, she had buoyed the image of his father's character and his culture. She was a wholehearted advocate of the civil rights movement sweeping the American South and an avid fan of Dr. Martin Luther King's speeches. She lionized the likes of

Reverend King and Supreme Court Justice Thurgood Marshall, swooned over black entertainers, and reveled in the rhythms of African music that reverberated in American culture. She had consciously and unconsciously instilled Black Pride in Barry's early life and taught him, as he put it, "To be black was to be the beneficiary of a great inheritance, a special destiny, glorious burdens that only we were strong enough to bear."

Years after he made the self-defining definition, Barack Obama said in a nationally broadcast radio interview that being of mixed-race was not alone the crucial issue in his self-definition. Having an African name had also made him stand out as a youngster. Like the protagonist of the song "A Boy Named Sue," who was given a name that was sure to make him a fighter, Barry's East African name stiffened his mettle. "When I was an awkward teen, the trouble I had didn't have to do with being black," he said. In retrospect, he said, being part black was "always positive." His early identity problem had less to do with his face than with his "funny name," he said. He observed that, as a teenager, "you always want to fit in. You wish your name was Tim Smith."

Religion was not a part of the Obama/Soetoro 'ohana in Honolulu. Speaking on the subject, candidate Obama said he was not raised in a particularly religious household. "My father, who I didn't know, returned to Kenya when I was just two. He was nominally a Muslim since there were a number of Muslims in the village where he was born. But by the time he was a young adult, he was an atheist. My mother, whose parents were non-practicing Baptists and Methodists, was one of the most spiritual souls I ever knew. She had this enormous capacity for wonder and lived by the Golden Rule. But she had a healthy skepticism of religion as an institution. And as a consequence, so did I." It was not until his life took a more serious turn toward helping others that he turned to Christianity.

Soetoro-Ng, whose father was Indonesian and whose husband is Chinese-Canadian, told Deborah Solomon of the *New York Times* that she thought of herself as "a half-white, half-Asian hybrid" who is philosophically a Buddhist. It was fine for her brother Barry to call himself black, she said, because "that is how he named himself. Each of us has a right to name ourselves as we will." Soetoro-Ng credits her free-thinking, multicultural mother for helping her children see that they could define themselves any way they wanted.

Soetoro-Ng remembers her mother telling them that even if you are not born to it, any culture can belong to you if you have sufficient love and respect for it. Barry and Soetoro-Ng credit both Hawai'i and Indonesia for who they are today. Their mother told them: "You can be anything you want to be," and she meant it, Soetoro-Ng said.

This matter of deciding what one is came up repeatedly as Hawai'i keenly followed Barack Obama's meteoric rise to prominence in the primary campaign. In the Islands he was embraced as a native son, and despite his personal racial preference, he was seen, in the Islands, as *hapa*. People in Hawai'i wanted him to proclaim himself *hapa*.

Honolulu publicist Elissa Josephson wondered aloud why the Democratic candidate did not do more to highlight his mixed race. "I wrote a letter to Barack Obama, asking him why he does not describe himself as *hapa*, and never got an answer," Josephson said. "To my thinking, it would be an asset for him to acknowledge in himself the unity of the races, the melding of the black and white cultures."

Professor Ronald Takaki of the Ethnic Studies Department at the University of California, Berkeley, also pondered the prospects of Obama as a candidate of ethnic multiplicity. Takaki grew up in the multiethnic neighborhood of Pālolo, a few miles from where Barry lived. As a child, Takaki would spend time in the homes of his Japanese, Chinese, Portuguese and Hawaiian neighbors, who used pidgin as their common language. Though no one ethnic group comprised a majority, it was only natural that living in America, many would compare themselves to what Takaki calls the master narrative of white, Eurocentric Americans. Like Barry Obama, Takaki left Hawai'i after high school to attend college on the Mainland, and like Obama, he took away a Hawai'i-inspired perspective on what America was and what it could be.

Takaki says that the monochromatic master narrative of his youth has been challenged by the ever-expanding diversity of the American people, personified in 2008 by Barack Obama's candidacy, which Takaki calls "a Manifest Destiny of diversity." In an op-ed piece expressing early support for candidate Obama, Takaki wrote: "He has made his complexion an American one, and his name an American-sounding one. He has opened a new identity not only for African-Americans, but also for Asian-Americans and Latino-Americans. As the son of a father from Kenya, he has remembered his immigrant roots; as the son of a Caucasian mother, he has represented mixed-race complexity. Like Tiger Woods, Obama has inspired biracial and multiracial Americans everywhere to embrace their ethnic multiplicity."

But has Obama done enough to make the case that he is of two races? Obama has acknowledged in stump speeches that his father was African and his mother white, but he could have taken another giant step, Takaki said.

"I wish Barack Obama would highlight the biraciality, the ethnic multiplicity, the cross-culturality of his identity."

According to Takaki, identity was something inherited, and also something invented. "Obama is not simply black," he argued. "Neither are about 80 percent of African-Americans. Even Alex Haley, the author of *Roots*, traced his ancestry only to Africa and not to Ireland. In his book *A Different Mirror: A History of Multicultural America*, Takaki notes that America is unique in having the "one-drop rule" that defines anyone who is part black as being black, while in other cultures, including that of South Africa and Latin America, "racial mixture is acknowledged, recognized." Because of America's history of slavery, he argues, communal acceptance of racial mixture was denied, erased in society.

As a candidate, a political leader, and even more so as president, Obama could bring about a change in how America looks at race by encouraging a new, more complicated, more accurate and open definition, Takaki has argued. "Obama has the opportunity to challenge and 'change' this tragic and insidious 'one-drop' rule by proclaiming his *hapa* identity. This is the reality for most African-Americans and certainly also for most Latinos, and also for an inclining population among Asian Americans."

Dr. Amy Agbayani, who has followed racial discrimination and affirmative action issues at the University of Hawai'i since the '70s, argues instead that in Hawai'i people of mixed-race backgrounds feel free to shift their alliances when it suits them. "It's not who you are, it's when you are," says Agbayani. "In Hawai'i, people are extremely aware of their various ethnic backgrounds. Even a little six-year old can tell you that she's part-Hawaiian, part-Filipino and part-Chinese." People in Hawai'i subconsciously pick the part of their identity that is best for a particular social or work situation, she notes. "It's like being bilingual, you know when to switch. If you're part-Portuguese you can be Portuguese when you're with your Portuguese family. If you're half-Filipino, you can be Filipino with the Filipinos, or switch mannerisms and act *haole*. It may not even be conscious. It's functional." Hawai'i's many successful mixed-race politicians and prominent businessmen don't play on their being *hapa*, says Agbayani. "No one knows how to be *hapa*. The term is 'local.' The important thing for a Hawai'i candidate is to relate to local." That's how the nation's first governor of Filipino ancestry, Ben Cayetano, got elected, she argues. "He didn't run as a Filipino. He ran as a local." When in Hawai'i, Barack Obama learned that lesson as well, she said. "There weren't black uncles around for him, almost none," she said. "But he knows instinctively how to relate to local."

For Barry's Kansas-born mother, Asia was the place to be because she believed that was where she could make a difference. After three years of research, she decided to return to Indonesia to learn more and do more and be more. Maya would attend the Jakarta International School, and Ann suggested that if Barry wanted, he could go there, too. But Barry decided to stay behind in Honolulu—even if it meant going back to live with Gramps and Toot—so that he could continue at Punahou. Ann consented. Gramps and Toot agreed to have him, as long as he promised not to flash his angst around the apartment.

It was not an easy decision for any of them, Soetoro-Ng recalled, but the overriding factor in everyone's mind was that Barry wanted to stay at Punahou with his friends and he felt comfortable there. That was really "all that mattered," Soetoro-Ng said.

Ann Soetoro left Hawai'i in 1977 and embarked on an academic and professional odyssey that would take her and her daughter through the Indonesian archipelago and on to Pakistan, China and Africa. More than many of her generation, she broke barriers for herself and people all over the world. When she wasn't working, she and daughter Maya traveled. They followed the ancient Silk Road to China, soaking in history and culture. "She was a globetrotter," Soetoro-Ng said. By her daughter's count, Ann Soetoro lived in 13 countries and found something to love in all of them. "She saw only the good in each place."

She eventually returned to Hawai'i for further study and research supported by the East-West Center. Her 1992 doctoral dissertation on Indonesian ironworkers—entitled *Peasant Blacksmithing in Indonesia: Surviving and Thriving Against All Odds*—swelled to 800 pages. The name on her dissertation is Stanley Ann Dunham. No longer just a dreamer, Dr. Dunham, the cultural anthropologist, became a no-nonsense expert in micro-financing and rural development. She broke barriers, as her mother did before her, but on a global scale, joining institutions that could be mobilized to help women and their poor brethren in places like Indonesia and Pakistan. She became associated with the People's Bank of Indonesia, the Agricultural Development Bank of Pakistan, the Women's World Bank of New York, and worked as a consultant to the U.S. Agency for International Development, the Ford Foundation and the World Bank.

She became precisely the internationalist that the East-West Center had hoped to produce. ℭℜ

CHAPTER EIGHT

"A CLIMATE OF MUTUAL RESPECT"
HAWAI'I IN THE '70S

In the '70s visitors were flocking to the Aloha State by the hundreds of thousands on affordable vacation packages made possible by an abundance of seats on ever-larger aircraft. The Jet Age had matured with the launch of the Boeing 747 Jumbo Jet in 1970. Hawai'i's tourism numbers had reached the million-visitors-a-year milestone in 1967, and thanks in part to the Jumbo Jet, the tourism turnstile took more than two million turns in 1972. Faster than you could say "passion fruit orange guava," Hawai'i had become a mass-market vacation option, a place where your neighbors and their lucky kids would go to buy *puka*-shell necklaces from the Philippines or wild and crazy tiki statues that made a mockery of the Hawaiian culture. No one could tell by looking at tiki bottle openers and other touristy trifles, but throughout Polynesia, the *tiki* is revered as godlike and is believed to have a spirit that should not be trifled with.

Media images had conditioned generations of Americans to think of Hawai'i as an exotic locale where *hula* girls swayed in grass skirts under a tropical moon and people lived without a care in grass huts, growing fat on a diet of pineapple and poi. Far from the reality of the Mainland, Hawai'i was a place where celebrities frolicked in the surf with buff beachboys and girls in bikinis. The sun was always shining and no one ever seemed to do any real work there. Hollywood did its part to foster the Islands' happy-go-lucky, *'ukulele*-playing image. It was no coincidence that Elvis Presley made three mindless Hawai'i-themed movies, *Blue Hawaii*, *Paradise Hawaiian Style* and *Girls! Girls! Girls!* without much planning or thought as to details like plot or relevance.

Hollywood churned out a few slightly more realistic dramas as well, including *Donovan's Reef*, *The Hawaiians* and *Hawaii*, the last based on James Michener's all-encompassing semi-historical novel. Surf movies enhanced Hawai'i's image as home of world-class waves. These included *Barefoot Adventure* and *Endless Summer*. TV also played a role, with much-watched weekly series like *Hawaiian Eye*, *Fantasy Island* and the iconic *Hawaii Five-O*.

This last remained popular week after week, even though it always consisted of nearly 50 minutes of cops talking about robbers until Steve McGarrett and his boys finally got in their car and chased the bad guys over scenic coastal highways before nabbing and booking them. Hawai'i people were sometimes a bit sore when Jack Lord and James MacArthur got all the credit for making the series a success, ignoring the contributions of local guys Kam Fong, a Chinese-American raised in Hawai'i who was a former Honolulu policeman, and Zulu, the Native Hawaiian actor who played Kono. Others were not pleased with the unflattering, crime-ridden image of the Islands created by the long-running series that somehow, inexplicably, attracted tourists.

The soundtrack for Hawai'i in the American mindset through the '60s consisted largely of the melodic marimba and pedal-steel guitar music of Martin Denny with a background of ersatz bird calls, an Afro-Caribbean sound that had little to do with the music Hawaiians were playing. Prior to the pedal-steel sound of the '50s and '60s, there was a long-established pop music tradition of sugary-sweet *hapa-haole* tunes. These *hula*-rhythm melodies with English-language lyrics tantalized America in the '20s, '30s and '40s. Many of the songs were written and recorded or played live by Hawaiians like Albert "Sunny" Cunha and Johnny Noble, while others were written by hack Tin Pan Alley tunesmiths.

In the '60s and early '70s, a few Hawaiians, including Alfred Apaka, Kui Lee and Don Ho, made their own kind of music that was heard on the Mainland. It would be a few more years before Hawaiian music was rejuvenated by a slew of new artists and record labels. All in all, the word was out that Hawai'i was a wonderful place for family tourism, with fine weather and the nation's most delicious tap water. And despite what TV watchers saw on *Hawaii Five-O*, it was a place that enjoyed a tranquil sense of security and safety. It was a tourism destination where you could use U.S. money, speak English and still experience the romance of overseas travel. No other state required visitors to fill out a Customs-like form before arrival. Eleven of the world's 13 climate zones were represented, from snow-capped mountain peaks to tropical rainforests. And the people were exotic too, known for their warm, welcoming spirit, their legendary kindness and laid-back "hang-loose" attitude; and after seeing racks of calendars in the bookstore and drugstore, one could not deny the physical beauty of the varied landscape and the smiling, golden-skinned men and women of the Islands.

After factoring out military families, the Hawaii Health Surveillance Study determined that by mid-1975 four ethnic groups each comprised more than 10 percent of the population: the Japanese constituted 31.8 percent; Caucasians, 20.8 percent; part-Hawaiians, 18.9 percent; and Filipinos, 10.5 percent.

The survey counted just 409 Negroes, accounting for one-tenth of one percent; although if the military families had been considered, the Negro population would have climbed to 8,000, according to the state statistician. At the time, there was talk that Native Hawaiians were a dying breed, numbering fewer than 10,000 and accounting for only 1.4 percent of the population of their native land.

An account in the *Honolulu Sunday Star-Bulletin & Advertiser*, entitled "Hawaii Super-Mixed by Interracial Marriage," said that about 50 percent of marriages involving Hawai'i residents in the year 1973 were interracial. Staff Writer Leonard Lueras wrote: "If marriage statistics are a social indicator, Hawaii's various ethnic groups must love each other a lot." George Tokuyama, the state's Registrar of Vital Statistics, said that he could not cite comparable statistics, but it was safe to assume that Hawai'i's interracial marriage rate was the world's highest.

Typically, Hawai'i's beauty queens and calendar-worthy lifeguards and firefighters are of mixed race. Some long-standing beauty pageants in the Islands are organized as fund-raising and scholarship events perpetuating a particular cultural tradition, such as the Japanese community's Cherry Blossom Queen, the Chinese community's Narcissus Queen and the Miss Hawai'i Filipina Pageant. Even so, it's not unusual for the young women pursuing these titles to be of mixed race, and it is more the rule than the exception that Miss Hawai'i candidates trace their ancestry to multiple races.

Popular in the '70s when Barry was in middle school was a novelty song called "Mister Sun Cho Lee," by a Hawaiian musician named Keola Beamer. The song makes fun of individuals who exhibit stereotypical character traits of their ethnicities, including Chinese, Filipino, Hawaiian and *haole*. But in the end the pidgin-flavored lyrics conclude: "One thing dat I know about dis place, all us guys we tease da oddah race / It's a wonder we all live in da same place." Local writer Rita Ariyoshi says the ethnic joke in the Islands acknowledges that Hawai'i's people know each other well and appreciate each other. Ariyoshi points out that they not only manage to live together in a very small place in the middle of nowhere; they also recognize and enjoy that this small place is a place that they share. The ultimate message of the ethnic joke in Hawai'i, she writes, is: "We are family and this is our home."

Barry Obama would have become easily aware of the mish-mash of names and colors and cultural qualities that blend together to become known as "local." In the '70s, his peers who were born in the '60s were beginning to take new interest in the things they had taken for granted: Hawaiian food, Hawaiian music, the Hawaiian language, Hawaiian values. In the mid-'70s, the tradition of May Day as Lei Day, a de rigueur annual event for every schoolchild in Hawai'i, took on a new mantle under which authenticity —flower *lei*, not paper or plastic *lei*—mattered. *Lū'au*, those Hawaiian-food feasts thrown on the occasion of a baby's first birthday or other auspicious events, took on new reverence as cultural happenings and not just family events. The University of Hawai'i took on a new responsibility and endeavored to be more respectful of and involved with the host culture: Henceforth it would take Hawaiian Studies seriously, a big step for a university that just a decade earlier had offered Hawaiian as a "foreign language." More than a century earlier, the missionaries had accomplished their goal of demeaning the Hawaiian culture, and nearly all the non-Christian values and traditions that went with it. An 1896 law formally banned the Hawaiian language from use in the public schools. *Hula* and Hawaiian chant, which had been used to hand down historical and cultural messages, were suppressed for generations. Over the decade of the '70s, that history of repression was soundly rejected in what many have now come to believe was nothing less than a cultural revolution.

Sometimes called the Hawaiian Renaissance, this cultural awakening brought new energy, enthusiasm and respect for authentic Hawaiian tradition. Cultural icons like *kumu hula* 'Iolani Luahine, Edith Kanakaole and Nona Beamer, who had quietly kept *hula* and other Hawaiian arts alive, were brought to the forefront and celebrated. Hawaiian music suddenly became hip and fresh. By extolling their Hawai'i roots with new verve and energy, local musicians broke the "export music" chains imposed by Mainland producers and impresarios and began writing, producing, recording and performing music for local audiences. There was marked new interest in traditional Hawaiian music like the slack-key styling of Gabby "Pops" Pahinui, and at the same time, new Hawai'i artists and groups came to the forefront, including the Beamer Brothers, Country Comfort, Olomana, Kalapana, the influential Sunday Manoa and the mixed-race duo Cecilio & Kapono. These and others claimed huge chunks of airtime on local Top 40 radio stations. In 1978, the Hawai'i Academy of Recording Arts handed out the first Nā Hōkū Hanohano Awards, the local equivalent of a Grammy that would recognize and honor Hawai'i artists and Hawai'i's music.

In another outward sign of Hawaiian pride, Punahou School graduate Nainoa Thompson, who was three years ahead of Barry Obama, was instrumental in reviving the ancient art of navigating a simple sailing canoe over great ocean distances. The launch of the double-hulled *Hōkūle'a* on a non-instrument trip to Tahiti in 1976 engendered pride in Hawai'i's Polynesian heritage among people of every race in the Islands.

Well-settled class and race assumptions were being challenged in popular culture, in politics and in a particularly Hawaiian rethinking about the idea of ethnic identity. Gone was the notion that Hawaiians were a dying race. Hawai'i residents of all ethnicities began to reassert their cultural pride. At the same time, growth as a threat to the fragile environment of Hawai'i had become a commanding issue. Environmental groups emerged and became militant in reaction to the rampant development that characterized the booming '60s and '70s in the Islands. Hawai'i had succeeded economically. Some now wondered loudly and publicly if it had succeeded too well. Battles were launched to save natural areas and popular beaches, including Sandy Beach along O'ahu's Ka 'Iwi shoreline, a favorite bodysurfing spot for Barry and his buddies.

The cultural or ethnic renaissance emerged out of many separate issues. The rise of black consciousness on the Mainland was a lesson heard in the Islands. Some sought to capture the energy of the Black Power movement, but with a particularly Hawaiian twist. Ethnic pride seized the imagination of a generation of young local people who traced their roots to immigrants from Japan, the Philippines and elsewhere who had come to work the sugar and pineapple plantations. This generation broke from parents who were far more concerned with assimilation and their own economic success than they were with explorations of self-identity. At the University of Hawai'i, a Department of Ethnic Studies emerged in 1970 with the mandate to provide research and service on the issues of race, culture and class. The program gained permanent status in 1977 and was deeply popular as a field of study for Island-born youngsters.

And something else emerged: a fresh new kind of ethnic identity that was particular to Hawai'i at the time but has since spread across the United States, particularly on the West and East Coasts. Hawai'i was among the first places to recognize and endorse a cultural awareness that went beyond specific ethnic groups to a broader pride in being what people in the Islands called "local." That is, non-white and from Hawai'i. It was a cross-cultural phenomenon that particularly prized people who were, in the Hawaiian word, *hapa*, of mixed race.

In earlier years, the term "local," if it was used at all, had a somewhat derogatory tone. At best, it distinguished Island people from Mainlanders. But by the late '60s and then fully by the '70s, "local" took on a new meaning, became a word filled with pride. In a paper written as a senior thesis, Eric Yamamoto—now a law professor—sought to explain how "local" became fraught with meaning:

"When one speaks about the Japanese, Chinese, Hawaiians or Filipinos in Hawai'i, he is not talking about separate ethnic units whose communities do not have interactions with each other. Rather, one must speak of a shared Island heritage of cultural background and lifestyle," he wrote. In the language of sociologists, this is a "polycultural" phenomenon, or a culture in which people are able "to live and participate in a mixed culture comfortably, understanding and sharing some cultural aspects of other cultural groups," Yamamoto wrote. Some believe the rise of "localism," which involved large numbers of young people with Japanese ancestry, was in part a reaction to negative feelings about investors and tourists from Japan who were buying up the state at a record pace. "We are not Japanese," the thinking went; "we are 'local,' with our own cultural identity and traditions."

Localism meant creating a culture in which one did not exist and then finding pride in that discovery. Localism even took a political form. In the late '70s, a pamphlet titled "Palaka Power," named after the sturdy plaid or calico shirt often worn by plantation workers, argued that locals had to organize and weave together as one strong cloth against what was seen as the overwhelming influence of Mainland corporations, Mainland media and Mainland ideas.

Its author, local lawmaker David Hagino, who felt others were using Palaka Power to oversimplify and stereotype a rather complex worldview, soon disowned it. But the enduring contribution of the Palaka Power movement and others like it was not, as some saw it at the time, a way to divide people. Rather, it was part of an understanding that Island-born-and-bred values were important and worth protecting as Hawai'i became more and more like the rest of the country. In many ways, it was a youthful reaction to a less-confident attitude held by previous generations of locally born residents—an attitude once famously observed by the late Gov. John A. Burns as a "subtle inferiority of spirit" among his local-born friends and political supporters.

But if ethnic awareness was alive in Hawai'i's young people, the phenomenon was particularly powerful for the state's host culture, the Hawaiians. After generations of subtle and not-so-subtle repression, Hawaiians were claiming their rightful place as proud *kānaka maoli*, or native people, within the larger society. These efforts soon took their own political turn as Hawaiians began demanding reparations for losses suffered through the overthrow of the Hawaiian monarchy in 1893. They began a process of self-determination that many hoped one day might lead to the rebirth of a sovereign Hawaiian "nation."

Today, the Hawaiian self-determination movement operates on many fronts. For some, the emphasis is on cultural values, including Hawaiian language-immersion schools. For others, it is economic empowerment. And for yet others, it is political recognition, either as an independent nation or even kingdom, or for recognition by the federal government as expressed in the Hawaiian political recognition legislation, or Akaka Bill, named for its key sponsor, Hawai'i Senator Daniel K. Akaka, a Chinese-Hawaiian.

On the other hand, when a *hapa* association was formed on the Mānoa campus to discuss such pressing issues as feelings of isolation or discrimination, members found that there weren't any. They soon disbanded and sent the money they had collected in dues to an Amerasian relief organization assisting *hapa* kids in Vietnam. But if the idea of *hapa* had become ingrained in Hawai'i and increasingly valued on the Mainland, it still posed problems for Island students who headed off to the Mainland for school and work. "It can lead to a kind of fetishism where we're seen as exotic," a young Chinese-Hawaiian student told her Mainland school newspaper.

Perhaps the single most dramatic incident in the rise of Hawaiian nationalism was the struggle to stop the bombing on the barren and windswept island of Kaho'olawe and reclaim it for Hawaiians. Uninhabited Kaho'olawe, clearly visible from the tourist resorts along the Maui coastline, was culturally significant to Hawaiians. But it was significant only at a distance. The island had long been used as a Navy practice bombing range and site for live-fire training. It was off limits to unauthorized civilians. The struggle to reclaim Kaho'olawe began on January 3, 1976, when a group of Hawaiians occupied the island in defiance of the U.S. Navy. After years of struggle, heartbreak and negotiation, the Navy finally stopped the bombing and relinquished the island. Today, Kaho'olawe is slowly healing as it waits to become the responsibility of a Hawaiian nation, when and if that entity emerges.

If Kaho'olawe was a struggle about culture and ethnic heritage, it was also a battle about land. Indeed, the '70s was a time in Hawai'i when public consciousness seemed to be dominated by land struggles, protests about development and a mounting concern about threats to Hawai'i's environment. It was an inevitable backlash against the wild years of development triggered by Statehood.

Put another way, the '70s was a time when Hawai'i engaged in a raging public and political conversation about growth and the reaction to growth. On the lush and rain-soaked Windward side of O'ahu, small farmers and Hawaiians fought to preserve two spectacularly beautiful valleys, Waiahole and Waikane, which had been planned for residential subdivisions. They were joined in their protest, interestingly enough, by energized students from the newly created Ethnic Studies program at UH who saw a lifestyle worth preserving. The struggle, which appeared hopeless at first, finally triumphed when the state generated huge headlines with word that it would spend millions to buy the disputed properties to "keep the country, country."

On the other side of O'ahu, along the dry and rocky coastline south of the tourist enclave of Waikīkī and not far from Henry Kaiser's pink suburbia, another battle arose. Development was planned on the coast overlooking the bone-crunching shore break popular with body surfers known as Sandy Beach. It was a beach Obama knew well. He and his pals would escape to "Sandys" on weekends to bodysurf, hang out and escape the weekday pressures of Punahou. It was also a beach Obama made sure to visit in later years when he would return to the Islands to visit his family on holidays.

A grassroots organization called Save Sandy Beach emerged to energize thousands of ordinary citizens in a political and petition battle against the planned development. This battle, like the one over Waiahole and Waikane Valleys, was eventually won when the city stepped in to rezone the property and preserve the open space around the popular surf spot. In many of these cases, such as the fight to preserve Waipahu's Ota Camp, an old plantation village, the battle was characterized as being about preserving a lifestyle as well as saving the land.

In a related way, the land struggles, particularly the occupation of Kaho'olawe, reminded people of the painful losses Hawaiians had experienced and the driving need to make things right, or *pono*, once again. The steady march of development led to a counterforce. Environmental groups such as Life of the Land (which takes its name from the state motto: "The Life of the Land Is Perpetuated in Righteousness") emerged as effective voices against out-of-control growth and environmental ruin. Young people flocked to the group or stood with Hawaiians and others on the barricades put up in protest against development. Punahou was not the only school to form environmental clubs eager to join in the cause.

Culturally, environmentally and socially, Hawai'i was on the move. Obama has said that his consciousness of the environment today was built by his years in Hawai'i, where the state's natural beauty was very publicly loved and threatened at every turn.

"Fairly early on, growing up in Hawai'i, not only do you appreciate the natural beauty, but there is a real ethic of concern for the land that dates back to the Native Hawaiians," Obama once said. "So it was natural for me, I think, growing up, to be concerned about these issues in a way now I think is common across the country but was more deeply embedded in Hawai'i at the time."

Deeply embedded indeed. In 1974, with Obama about to embark on his high school years, a campaign for governor hinged on this very issue. The previous Democratic governor, Burns, had become associated, rightly or wrongly, with the development excesses that accompanied Hawai'i's spectacular post-Statehood growth. His legacy was under challenge by Thomas P. Gill, a former congressman and lieutenant governor whose campaign was built around the idea that it was time to bring some of the worst excesses of growth and development under control. Gill lost to Burns' handpicked successor, George R. Ariyoshi, but the lesson of the challenger was not lost. Ariyoshi became closely associated with the idea of growth control and, indeed, was the individual responsible for the state's decision to buy those two lush Windward O'ahu valleys.

Much of the ferment of the time landed squarely at the 1978 Constitutional Convention, a "peoples' convention" that met in Honolulu the summer before Barry's senior year at Punahou. The convention embedded idealistic environmental and social dreams deep into the state Constitution itself. After the voters approved it, the new Constitution granted sweeping protections for Hawai'i's land and water resources and formally recognized traditional Hawaiian access rights and gathering practices. It made Hawaiian an official state language. A lasting outgrowth of the 1978 "Con Con" was the creation of the state's Office of Hawaiian Affairs, a semiautonomous branch of government that gave formal recognition to the role of the Hawaiian people in identifying and managing their own resources. The office, charged generally with working for "the betterment of the Hawaiian people," would use income shared from former Hawaiian Kingdom government and crown lands, now held in trust by the state, to provide grants and loans and other financial benefits for persons who could show they had some Hawaiian blood. All of a sudden, there were more than bragging rights associated with being of Hawaiian blood, or *koko*; there were entitlement programs. Decades later, when the fad for "Got Milk?" labels took off, Hawaiians came up with a bumper sticker that asked, "Got Koko?"

In the years since, the Office of Hawaiian Affairs has been the target of many lawsuits that argued its programs and objectives are race based and thus constitutionally impermissible. At least one case (*Rice v. Cayetano*) made it all the way to the Supreme Court, where justices ruled against a Hawaiians-only voting and eligibility requirement. Ultimately, the fate of all such Hawaiian-focused programs will be decided by Congress and, most likely, the administration of the next president.

In the '70s, however, those legal challenges were a distant thought. In the wake of the Hawaiian Renaissance, it was good to be Hawaiian and part-Hawaiian. Many of those people who had been describing themselves as part-Chinese or part-Japanese were now calling themselves part-Hawaiian instead. The Census began to see a surge in the number of people who defined themselves as Hawaiian, either out of sheer pride or because they were measuring the benefit of federal and state entitlements for Hawaiians.

In short, the '70s was a time of sweeping social change in the Islands. Even after seven generations of missionary influence, Punahou was not immune. Obama and most of his classmates might not have been actively involved in this rebirth of Hawaiian pride and activism and the larger context of a new style of Island-bred ethnic and cultural awareness. But they couldn't escape it. It was part of the music they listened to, the news they heard on radio and television or read in the newspapers. It was, in a very real sense, part of the very air they breathed. It would have been impossible for a young person growing up in Hawai'i at the time not to have felt some impact from the intertwined threads of ethnic awareness, Hawaiian cultural pride and environmental urgency. "I thought about him," said Obama's former teacher Pal Eldredge. "It was everyone's racial renaissance and he was smack in the middle of it."

As a Hawai'i-born high school student, Barry Obama embarked on a different cultural discovery. While he sought information and insight into what it meant to be black, his own self-definition, he came to appreciate Hawai'i as a place where people of many cultures and backgrounds live in harmony, learn about each other and learn to live with each other.

It was said of him by his half-sister that growing up in Hawai'i gave Barry "a sense that a lot of different voices and textures can sort of live together, however imperfectly."

In the end he realized that Hawai'i has too many races for any of them to rule the roost and in this way, political and economic power is split among them. Or, as Abercrombie says, often in the context of campaigning for Obama, "Diversity defines us but doesn't divide us." ❧

CHAPTER NINE

"AN INCUBATOR FOR THE ISLAND ELITES"
PUNAHOU SCHOOL,
MICROCOSM OF HAWAI'I

When Barry Obama joined the Class of 1979, there were few African-Americans among Punahou's 1,200 students. Years after graduating from high school, the civil rights lawyer and politician Barack Obama described Punahou as "an incubator for Island elites." Though it was and is the choice of the Island's over-achievers, and though it continues to offer preference in admissions to descendants of missionaries six or seven generations after its founding, the institution has been no stranger to issues of race and equal opportunity. From its inception and down through the decades, Punahou's leaders were keenly aware of both the baser sentiments that attach to race relations and the higher calling of an educational community to strive for integration and equal opportunity.

The Punahou School started small in 1841 and, like the missionary families behind it, grew prosperous over the decades of change. In 1829, Hawai'i's strong-willed Queen Ka'ahumanu, who had once ordered the missionaries to leave the Islands, did an about-face. She urged O'ahu's Governor Boki to give some land to the Reverend Hiram Bingham in support of the Sandwich Island mission. The Queen, who became a Christian, kept a thatched hut on the Punahou lands and saw to it that a hut was built nearby for the Binghams. At the time, the land was on the outskirts of civilization. The Queen commanded that a rock wall be built to keep roaming royal cattle out of the settlement. The wall was made of dry rock stacked five feet high. Part of it still marks the school's boundary, still topped by the cactus-like night-blooming cereus planted by Mrs. Bingham, which erupts in yellow and white blossoms in summer.

It is widely assumed that the missionaries who founded Punahou were only interested in educating their own children. That's not the case, as the missionary band's first efforts were aimed at raising native Hawaiians "to an elevated state of Christian civilization." Their next project was the Punahou School, which eliminated the need to send the missionaries' children back to New England for their education. Parting with their children at age six, consigning them to a life as veritable orphans, proved too painful for their parents. Though it might have made sense to combine the earliest school for Hawaiians with the school for missionary children, it was out of the question. The idea of integrated education had been tried in Tahiti 20 years earlier but abandoned when the Tahitian girls were found "entertaining" the young white men.

In the 1840s, there was no tuition at Punahou School, and no admission policy. Students simply showed up and remained enrolled in classes as long as they behaved as good Christian children. Younger kids were hauled by cart over the two miles that separated the school from the main mission at Kawaiaha'o in downtown Honolulu.

Older kids walked over the treeless plain in woolen clothes and hand-made boots or they walked barefoot, crushing caterpillars all along the way. Students from the outer islands boarded at the school, which also was a farm. An early map showed the school's three main buildings were surrounded by ball fields and pasture. Up by the Upper Pasture were the cow pen, milking pen, hen yard, horse paddock, banana and taro patches and vegetable gardens, as well as the servants' quarters. Closer to the Lower Pasture was the extensive cornfield. Male boarders were expected to rise at dawn and work the fields with hoes before breakfast. Female students did the cooking and mended the boys' clothes. The first school building was built of mud and grass scooped up from the hillside. The second building was a two-story affair built of stone blasted from Rocky Hill, which stood over the educational compound like a sentinel.

One tends to think of 19th-century missionary kids as strait-laced toe-the-liners. By 1854, the school had been opened up to the public, and some admission criteria and a standard of conduct policy were in place. Already by 1858, Punahou students were getting a rep, and not as goody-goody boys. W.D. Alexander of Maui, whose son was a boarding student, wrote to complain of a rumor that the boys were looking *under* the skirts of the girls as they climbed the stairs of the Old School.

Hawaiian students were admitted in the late 1850s, some on Government scholarships, and eventually one in 10 Punahou students was Hawaiian. In the early years, most of the *haole* missionary kids spoke some Hawaiian language.

Hawai'i-born Chinese students were admitted beginning in 1867. The first Japanese student had enrolled in 1883 when the Consul General's son was admitted. By 1896, the influx of Chinese students—26 out of 120 students—was causing concern among some of Punahou's supporters. Among those Chinese students who passed through Punahou were Sun Yat Sen, the founder of modern China. Sun received most of his Western education at 'Iolani School, another respected private institution in Hawai'i. But he then finished off at Punahou, also known at the time as O'ahu College.

In 1891 Punahou celebrated its 50th anniversary with another forward-looking speech by a distinguished son of Hawai'i missionaries and Punahou School, the Maui-born Civil War hero Samuel C. Armstrong. Years earlier, as a colonel commanding the 9th Regiment of United States Colored Troops, Armstrong helped found the Hampton Normal and Industrial Institute in Hampton, Virginia, to train freed slaves. Before the Emancipation Proclamation, teaching slaves, freed men or mulattoes to read or write was against the law in the Old Dominion. Learn they did at Hampton Institute, now known as Hampton University. Hampton went on to produce great educators like Booker T. Washington, and Armstrong went on to become a Brigadier General after leading the Colored Troops into battle against Confederate General Robert E. Lee's army in Virginia. In recognition of his contribution as an educator, Richmond, Virginia named a public elementary school after him and Punahou named Armstrong Hall for him. In his Jubilee Speech on the occasion of Punahou's 50-year anniversary, General Armstrong said he foresaw a time when Punahou would in time be known for academic excellence and attract "pupils from over the sea."

On the occasion of Punahou's 75th anniversary, Lorrin A. Thurston, the missionary descendant Punahou alumnus who was a key figure in the overthrow of the Hawaiian monarchy, provided an early defense of multiculturalism. While some people were championing segregation of the races, Thurston argued that abandoning "the policy of toleration and friendly association" and substituting a "policy of segregation, exclusion and aloofness" would damage the spirit in which Punahou was founded. "It will be a disaster to Hawai'i," he said in his 1916 speech. "Our duty is to give our Brother fair play and equal opportunity, and not attempt to fix his status by virtue of the color of his skin."

By the time the school marked its 150th anniversary, however, it had gained a hard-to-shake reputation as an institution by the *haole* and for the *haole*.

Twenty years after she graduated, 1970 Punahou School alumna Mindy Pennybacker was curious to know if students at public high schools had changed their perception of Punahou, which had been traditionally regarded as a school for "*haole* rich kids." Even though many changes had taken place at Punahou, it did not take Pennybacker long to learn that like Harvard and Yale, the prep school was still saddled with a reputation for being white as a bowl of steamed rice. Writing in a sesquicentennial anniversary book called *Punahou, the History and Promise of a School of the Islands,* Pennybacker recounted the school's history of *haole*-ism over the most recent half century. In 1944, 90 percent of students were *haole*. Twenty years later, in 1966, 69 percent were *haole*. By 1976, when Barry Obama was a sophomore, the percentage of *haole* had declined to about 60 percent. In 1984, that percentage dropped to 40, a dramatic decrease from earlier numbers, yet it remained higher than the 23-percent *haole* population in the state.

In her essay, Pennybacker revealed that Punahou had imposed an admission quota in the 1890s to limit the number of Asian students to 10 percent of the student body. When John Fenton Fox took charge as Punahou's president in 1944, he was ashamed of the Oriental Quota he had inherited because, he said, it was "un-Christian." But it would remain in effect as long as Punahou families kept up the pressure to keep the school from becoming overly Asian.

Punahou's 10-percent quota of the 1950s and 1960s was liberal compared to the Pacific Club, which was founded in 1851. The oligarchical white men's club, a mecca for dealmakers and cigar-smokers who met in "Gentlemen Only" rooms, banned Orientals from membership until 1968 and prevented women from becoming members until 1984.

By 1990, Punahou's Asian quota was gone but the school's admission preferences for children of alumni and children who were descended from the Christian missionary founders remained in place.

Dr. Siegfried Ramler, Punahou's head of curriculum development and instructional services, worked for both Fox and his successor, Rod McPhee. Ramler came to Hawai'i in 1951 fresh from the Nuremberg trials, where he'd served as an interpreter. As a Punahou teacher and administrator for 40 years, Ramler advocated continual expansion of foreign-language and history and culture area studies to reflect Hawai'i's ethnic mix and open the students' eyes to the world. Under Ramler, Punahou offered up to six years of study in Chinese, French, German, Japanese or Spanish, and shorter sequences in Hawaiian, Latin and Russian. Over the years, the Hawai'i school sought sister school relationships in Japan and China, established student exchange programs and brought fascinating speakers to campus from around the world.

Along with the expanded and outward-looking formal curriculum, Punahou's cultural milieu and Hawai'i's multiethnic social life contributed to what Ramler called a "hidden curriculum." Together, the formal and hidden curricula set the *weltanschauung* or worldview that would prepare youngsters to be world citizens. By encouraging participation and self-expression in an open academic environment, Punahou built self-esteem and the ability to express oneself in a multicultural world, something a bridge-building politician like Barack Obama would need. "I would like to think this milieu gave him many of the essential tools he would need in his later life," Ramler said.

One photo in a middle school yearbook of the time captures the moment. In front of a chalkboard with the phrase "Mixed Races of America" written on it, Obama poses with others, waving a peace sign for the camera. At the time, Barry Obama was undoubtedly like most students: focused on friends, family and the pleasures and stresses of school and growing up. But there was at least one place where Barry, like every Punahou student, was quite deliberately exposed to ideas beyond his own teenaged concerns. This was in the structured environment of the chapel, where the curriculum focused on the values of ethnic diversity, cultural awareness and environmental concern that were also so much a part of the public conversation in Hawai'i at the time.

Once every six days, students from grade school through high school were required to troop to Thurston Chapel for a non-denominational service rooted in Punahou's Christian heritage: Bible study and worship. Chapel sessions dwelt on all forms of Christianity as well as Buddhism, Baha'i, Islam and Judaism.

But by the '70s, chapel sessions had transformed into something much broader: Bible-based discussions and lessons on fundamental values and ethics. Central to those lessons were important Island values, including proper stewardship of the land (later to be known as *mālama 'āina*, or care for the land), respect for cultural diversity and social responsibility or caring for others. "It had always been one of the purposes of the chapel, to integrate these values in our services," said John Heidel, a Congregational minister who was lead chaplain at Punahou during Barry's years there. "It wasn't learning the books of the Bible. It was learning the values behind those stories."

In its determination to be diverse, the admissions process was designed to ensure that the student body would reflect the rainbow of cultures and races that made up Hawai'i. Thus "diversity was especially important," Heidel said. "People would be asked to trace their heritage and tell their different stories, but also learn to respect the stories of others." In retrospect, said Heidel, now retired, the emphasis was on the cultures and heritages that were the primary strains of Hawai'i's story: the Chinese, Japanese, Filipino, Caucasian and other ethnic groups who found their way to the Islands and—of course—the Hawaiians. "The idea of singling out African-Americans probably didn't come up. There were so few. That was the reason we didn't really go to the African-American experience that much. The others were top of mind," Heidel said.

Chapel was also a time to talk with Punahou students about the environment that surrounded them and the importance of respecting and protecting the land. "We would talk about the Creation story and where it talks about having dominion over the Earth and we'd ask: Does this mean to keep control or ownership of the land, or does it mean stewardship?" Heidel said. "I remember talking to the kids about establishing a proper relationship with the land. How do you have a proper relationship?"

While chapel lessons often spoke of the importance of preserving and protecting the land, a particularly important lesson in limited and fragile Hawai'i, Heidel said he does not think many students made the connection to direct political action—at least not at the time. College students in the '70s were valued foot soldiers in struggles such as those to save Kalama Valley on O'ahu's South shore, Sandy Beach, and Waiahole and Waikane Valleys. For most high school students, it was a somewhat different matter.

"I don't think many of the kids were activists at the time," Heidel said. But lessons planted then were expected to sprout later, he added. "I remember getting a letter from a student, now in his 40s [Obama's generation], thanking me. He said, 'It never dawned on me what I was hearing all those years and the diversity and what I was taught until now,'" Heidel recounted.

In fact, that letter-writing alumnus' experience illuminates what was a core objective of Punahou when Obama was a student and remains a central objective today: to plant life values that will take seed and grow over a lifetime. "The Punahou experience is very formative," Heidel said. "It's a deliberate thing. Teaching values was definitely part of our intentional curriculum in chapel. It was a very directed thing."

In addition to chapel, a nearby round classroom, the Roundhouse, used for religious studies, was inspired by Buddhism's bent for harmony. The school developed a community service program to ensure that students were not isolated in a tropical ivy tower. In a further effort to broaden the student base, Punahou put its money where its mouth was. Scholarships and partial scholarships like those that brought Barry to Punahou were awarded without regard to financial need. When Barry attended Punahou, tuition rose to about $1,900 a year, at a time when the average annual household income was under $23,000. Scholarships like his helped make the student body more representative of Hawai'i's racial breakdown, moving it beyond the "rich *haole*" demographic.

In later life, Obama recognized that there was more to school than going to class and playing basketball: "Certainly, there was an emphasis on values and ethics and being a good citizen, as well as a good student," he told a *Sports Illustrated* interviewer. "I didn't always observe these admonitions. But [that emphasis] has an impact on you. It gives you a sense of what you should be striving for. And even if you're rebelling from it, as I was during my teenage years, it still sunk in, and had a long-term impact on the trajectory of my life." ℘

CHAPTER TEN

"An overtly black game"
Barry O'Bomber, Reserve Forward

In a state with no major league teams in any sport, there was still a lot on the playing fields to capture Barry's attention. Hawai'i had a close connection to baseball in that Alexander Cartwright, who laid out the rules for what was to be the national pastime, had perfected the game in Honolulu in the 1850s. The Hawaii Islanders Pacific Coast League baseball franchise played home games at Honolulu Stadium, less than a mile from Gramps' apartment, until the termite-ridden structure was demolished in 1976 and the games were moved to the newly built Aloha Stadium.

Known by the team nickname "Rainbows," the University of Hawai'i football team was consigned to the junior division of collegiate competition until 1974, when the squad earned its colors as a Division I team. Barry took some interest in football and made the intermediate school team in the eighth grade. His coach on the gridiron was Pal Eldredge, who had been his math teacher in fifth grade. Barry respected Coach Pal as a no-nonsense Hawaiian who called things as he saw them. Even so, Barry was a little miffed when he didn't make the starting line-up, believing he was a better pass-catcher than the starting receivers.

But it was basketball that won Barry's heart and soul and helped shape his character. He didn't know the game when he arrived in Hawai'i from Indonesia. As it happened, he arrived in the Islands when the state was in a frenzy over the current UH team, dubbed the "Fabulous Five." The University of Hawai'i had been fielding basketball teams for nearly 60 years. In 1970, thanks to the Fab Five, the Hawai'i team emerged as a national powerhouse and took its phenomenal 23 wins–5 losses record to the National Invitational Tournament, giving the 50th State its first taste of national sports glory. The next year, the same five starters were back.

Everybody wanted to see the famous Fab Five: Al Davis, Jerome Freeman, Dwight Holiday, Bob Nash and John Penebacker. Tickets for games in the 1971-72 season were a hot item, but Gramps scored two for himself and Barry. Of particular interest to the wide-eyed boy at his first basketball game

91

was that all five of the Fab Five players were African-American kids from the Mainland. They had been recruited to come to Hawai'i to play ball, and play ball they did. Up to that moment, Barry had had little opportunity to observe black Americans. He was most impressed with the way the deft young athletes were adored by the cheering fans, and how they responded to the girls with winks and nods. Right then and there, he decided that he wanted to be part of that world. While Barry would choose to go on to the Mainland to find his place, several members of that famous team settled in Hawai'i, where they would become prominent in business, in labor and in politics.

Barry's father had given him a basketball the previous Christmas, and a year later, as a sixth-grader, Barry began shooting hoops in a playground near his apartment building. He recalls dribbling down to the court daily and getting tips from older kids. Once he started playing basketball, he never stopped. Decades later, during the campaign, he tried to take time out to play some hoops, sometimes with members of his Secret Service detail. On the morning of the Iowa Caucuses where he made his breakout political move in the young presidential campaign, Obama joined with several of his high school buddies, to be nicknamed the "Band of Brothers," for a ritual election-day pick-up game. Barry's middle school classmates recall that he always seemed to have a basketball in his hand, dribbling down the school's paths and corridors on the way to class, even on the way home from Foodland. As soon as he had matured as a player, he began looking for after-school pick-up games.

He practiced hard. He practiced long. When other kids took a juice break between classes at 10 a.m., he shot baskets. While others spent their lunch break talking in the lunchroom, Barry was in the gym. When it was time for many kids to ride around in their expensive cars, Barry was still shooting baskets. "Basketball was a good way for me to channel my energy," Obama would later recall. While in motion on the courts, he was constantly challenging himself, gaining confidence, working through stuff. "Basketball *was* a refuge, a place where I made a lot of my closest friends, and picked up a lot of my sense of competition and fair play. It was very important to me all the way through my teenage years," he said in an interview.

Obama's brother-in-law, Craig Robinson, a standout basketball player at Princeton, said basketball was central to Obama's discovery of who he was and what he could do. Robinson, who would become head coach at Brown and then Oregon State, told the *New York Times*: "He didn't know who he was until he found basketball. It was the first time he really met black people." He didn't just play against them; he studied them.

To survive socially in high school at Punahou, you had to be in a clique. Basketball would be Barry's clique. When he went out for the junior varsity basketball team in the 10th grade, it was as if, after five years of being an out-sider, he now belonged at Punahou. His family, friends and former teachers seemed to agree that Barry's happiest moments at Punahou were spent on the hardwood court of the gym or on the outside courts, mixing it up with his best friends and whomever he could get to play against him.

By the time he was in junior high school, the baby fat was gone. Barry was a lanky left-hander, a little over 6-foot-1, with a sensational jump shot and a tricky left-handed double-pump shot. "He would drive his whole body into you and then shoot a fade-away shot," said fellow court and playground player Richard Haenisch, who was a year behind Obama. The sheepish, shy kid had become a fierce competitor who idolized the high-spinning, hard-dunking Julius Erving of the NBA's Philadelphia 76ers.

In high school, he spent hours shooting baskets on the hardwood at the Neal Blaisdell Center arena, where the Punahou team practiced, and on the school's Upper Courts. But the real action for Barry was on the Lower Courts, which were open to public play after school hours. There he could get in on pick-up games frequented by basketball-obsessed 20- and 30-year-old guys from the workaday world who worked out their own frustrations under the hoops. The pick-up games at Punahou were spirited, especially on Friday evening and Saturday and Sunday afternoon. The two courts on Wilder Avenue were well known among basketballers in the community and the military, though not as famous for hot play as the Paki Park courts near the Waikīkī Fire Station. Some of the players were black, and in this way, basketball became one way for Barry to study and learn about being African-American. The rumble-tumble rat-ball pick-up games gave Barry a chance to practice a showier game and prove, to himself, at least, that he was a better player than some of the starters on his state championship team. Years later, when the Lower Courts were gone, Obama would show up at the Paki Park courts to spend a few hours of his holiday trips home.

Dan Hale, one of Barry's varsity teammates who also played pick-up ball, recalled: "There was a group of us gym-rat types, always looking for a game. Barack could play. He had a passion for it. He had a nice little running jumper in the lane, with his signature double-pump. If he missed, he'd be the first guy following his shot. If you left him open, he'd stick it, but he'd take you to the hoop, too." Alan Lum, another of Barry's teammates on the varsity team, remembers that Barry had great skill at making long shots. Lum said it was the speed and accuracy of Barry's shots that earned him the nickname Barry O'Bomber.

Basketball gave Barry a new lease on life and new friends who would be his closest in Hawai'i. Playing ball gave him a sense of accomplishment and achievement. There was instant satisfaction, he said, in making a great move against an opponent who thought he was pretty good and stuffing him. Barry earned respect that way, and it didn't matter where he came from or who his daddy was. It gave him his first dream of what he could become, of who he could be in this life. When Tony Peterson, who was two years ahead of him at Punahou, confided to Barry that he was planning to be a lawyer, Barry told him: "When you're a big-shot lawyer and I'm a basketball star, you can negotiate my NBA contract." Neither realized their first dream. Peterson became a preacher and Obama became a politician.

Hard as he tried, good as he was at basketball, Barry remained a reserve forward, never a starter, on the Punahou varsity teams that were destined to be state champions.

In his memoir, Obama put chip-on-the-shoulder words into the mouth of a friend who questioned whether race was a factor in both the football coach's and basketball coach's decisions to keep Barry on the bench when he was a better athlete than some of the starters. But in the words he attributed to himself, Obama surmised that he was a bench player on the school's champion basketball team because the others had learned to play "like white boys."

"I had an overtly black game," Obama remembered. That meant he went in for showboating behind-the-back passes and didn't care much about fundamentals like bounce passes. Teammate Lum, who later became a Punahou teacher and basketball coach, put it another way: "His game didn't really fit our system. We ran a structured offense. We were very disciplined," he said. Barry did okay with that, but he was "a very creative player," Lum said.

In fact, the 1979 varsity was a typically mixed-race Buffanblu team. Three of the starters were part-Hawaiians, one was a Filipino-American and Dan Hale, the 6-foot-7 star center, was *haole*. Race wasn't an issue in who started, Hale told the *New York Times*. As the only white kid among the starters, Hale said: "I had my own issues to worry about. Being a *haole* from Punahou, that's the worst."

According to Honolulu sports writer Dave Reardon, writing nearly 30 years later, Punahou's 1979 championship team boasted some of the best high school basketball players in Hawai'i. Barry would certainly have been a starter on any other team in the state. Barry's problem wasn't that he was black; it was that his game was black. Punahou's game came from the playbook. Barry's game came from the street.

Looking back, candidate Obama said his aggravation over not being a starter paralleled other bigger issues he was wrestling with. "There were some issues of racial identity that played themselves out on the basketball court," he said.

In May 2008, *Sports Illustrated* named Punahou School the nation's No. 1 high school for athletic sports programs. Barack Obama, who was driving hard for the title President of the United States, gave an interview to the nation's No. 1 sports mag, and the interviewer got right into the old question of why he wasn't a starter on Coach Chris MacLachlin's varsity team, the team that went on to beat Moanalua High School 60-28 to win the 1979 state championship.

"When I joined the high school team, there was some strain," Obama recalled. "Coach MacLachlin was a terrific coach, but he was also Mr. Fundamentals. He was very big on picks and rolls and bounce passes and chest passes. He never cared for behind-the-back passes or spin moves. So we had some conflict. We had some tension. In retrospect, I realize that he probably was right in most of our disagreements. At the time I thought he was unfair. But he was a terrific coach, we had a terrific team and we had some great players. I have very fond memories of our team."

Still, Obama told *SI* that he had made a difference on what was one of Punahou's best-ever basketball teams. "(In) my senior year, when we won the state championship, there were a couple games where I think I was a difference maker. I remember my grandfather, who'd listened to the broadcast of the game, telling me that the big sports announcer, sort of the Howard Cosell of Hawai'i, had said about me on television, 'Boy, this kid can really play.' It was good to get a few props late in life. But the truth is that my favorite memories had to do more with seeing our team do well."

He recalled with pride that he played on the team with John Kamana, the state's best athlete, who went on to play for USC on a football scholarship and play tight end for the Rams and Falcons; and he was two years behind another Buffanblu basketballer who went on to play in the NFL: Mark Tuinei, the "Gentle Giant" lineman of the Dallas Cowboys.

Obama said the larger lessons drawn from his high school basketball career were these: "I learned a lot about discipline, about handling disappointments, being more team-oriented, and realizing not everything is about you. Those are lessons that have stayed with me."

One thing about Barry all the other teammates remembered was that he wasn't afraid to make an argument for what he thought was the right thing to do. Like his father years before at those small African schools, Barry O'Bomber would court trouble by speaking up about the coaches' methods and decisions and say what other players were thinking but afraid to say.

That earned him respect. "He wasn't afraid to challenge authority," said teammate and friend Alan Lum.

Barack Obama acknowledged this gift, which he had perhaps inherited from his outspoken father. In an interview for *O, The Oprah Magazine*, he said: "I knew I could express myself. I knew I could win some arguments." Barry realized that the power of words could serve to unite as well as divide. "I learned very early on in Hawai'i how to bring people together," he said. ❧

CHAPTER ELEVEN

"A FITFUL INTERIOR STRUGGLE"
TURBULENT TIMES IN HIGH SCHOOL

Having defined himself as black, Barack Obama set out while still in high school to learn what it meant to be a black man in America. "Away from my mother, away from my grandparents, I was engaged in a fitful interior struggle," Obama said. "I was trying to raise myself to be a black man in America."

The problem was, Hawai'i did not have many black residents. With African Americans making up only three percent of the population, including transient military families, Hawai'i in the '70s was lacking in black cultural influences. Apart from the Fab Five basketball stars and the long-serving African-American politician Charles Campbell, Hawai'i didn't have that many African-American role models. Because the school he attended had so few blacks, Barry was like an Indiana Jones, a character based on Punahou graduate Hiram Bingham, who unearthed the ruins of Machu Picchu. He was actively searching for clues to uncover the treasured black identity he'd been hearing about.

In his book *Dreams*, Obama looked back on his days in high school as if he spent four years in a personal torture chamber. He described the agony of trying to find his identity as a black man in America when he was still living with a white family and dealing every day with rejection by a multiracial student body.

"I tried to raise myself as a black man in America, and beyond the given of my appearance, no one around me seemed to know exactly what that meant."

As part of his search, Barry got into the soulful singers Marvin Gaye and Stevie Wonder and the iconic, influential TV show *Soul Train*, which was as much an authority on the latest R&B hits and dance crazes as it was a showcase for the latest fashions and fads in the black community. Barry took courage from the exploits of Richard Roundtree, the *Shaft* actor who took black action movies to new heights and depths, and learned to curse from

Richard Pryor, the comic who set the bar high on lowdown dirty language.

Among his other tutors were the authors James Baldwin, W.E.B. DuBois, Ralph Ellison, Langston Hughes and Richard Wright, whose counsel he sought in the library. These teachers repudiated and validated the many things he was learning about the black experience in America.

But it was in the words of Malcolm X that Barry found a passage that related to something he himself was thinking and feeling. It was the passage where Malcolm discussed the white blood he had inherited from his maternal grandfather, an Englishman, who had impregnated his mother, described by Malcolm as his mother's shame. In *The Autobiography of Malcolm X*, the Black Muslim leader wrote that he wished the white blood that coursed through his veins could be expunged from him. It made Obama wonder what he would be if he could leave his mother and grandparents at some mythical frontier and go forward without them in his past.

Barry had experienced firsthand jabs about his blackness. In the seventh grade, he had even punched a kid in the nose after the kid called him a "coon." He never forgot how a tennis pro had made a remark about his blackness not being able to rub off, and how an assistant basketball coach, fresh-off-the-boat from New York, had used the word "niggers" to disparage the black players on an opposing team. Barry had also become uncomfortably class-conscious in a school where many of his classmates "had big homes and fancy cars of their own and were living much more lavishly than I was." He said he rarely met anyone less well off financially than he was.

In his high school years of exploration and exasperation, Barry desperately sought black companions who knew the anger and confusion he was experiencing, confidants who could fill him in on how to act in Hawai'i.

Being so few in number, the "brothers," as they called themselves, spent time hanging out together both at school and after school. They swapped stories about how other Punahou students, especially girls, acted around them and reacted to them. Basketball buddy Haenisch, a year younger and not a close friend, had a story that was remarkably similar to that of the future presidential candidate. Like Obama, Haenisch came from biracial parents. His mother was Yugoslavian and his father was an African-American military man who was missing-in-action in Vietnam. Richard Bradic spent his early years in Germany and, after his mother's death, he was adopted by a family friend who moved him to the Islands and gave him her last name. Haenisch arrived in the Islands as culturally confused as Barry. He barely spoke English when he first started school in Honolulu. As with Obama, basketball became the key to acceptance for the 6-foot-4 high school kid. "It was mostly the 'haves,' the Kāhala crowd who were well-off, and it was mostly *haole* when we were there," Haenisch told the *Honolulu Advertiser.* "Certainly blacks were not prevalent there at all."

Despite basketball, it was a challenging social time. "It was difficult to date," he recalled. "It was not socially acceptable yet, not in a black-and-white kind of thing. The *haole* girls liked the *hapa* boys or the Asian boys and vice versa. It was very difficult to like a girl and be seen with a black kid on campus unless he was some kind of star, athletically."

"Most blacks we came into contact with were Mainland blacks who were mostly bitter toward white people in general and they would transpose that to Hawai'i, which I don't think was fair," Haenisch said. "It was difficult, but not as difficult as it could be on the Mainland."

Haenisch, in fact, rose to national attention long before his older basketball-playing buddy. After high school, Haenisch went on to Chaminade University in Honolulu, where he played on the team that upset the No. 1 team in the nation, Virginia, and its No. 1-ranked player, Ralph Samson. It was the sports upset of the century for Hawai'i, and a photograph of Haenisch, sitting triumphantly in a basket following his team's improbable victory, was seen in newspapers across the country. After a brief stint in the pros, Haenisch became a successful financial planner in Los Angeles.

The older black students at Punahou had already introduced themselves to members of Honolulu's tight-knit African-American community. They got invited to parties where they would be with other blacks at the university and military bases on O'ahu. Obama's book describes the atmosphere of these parties, although his former classmates say he did not often go to them.

In 1975-76 when Barry was a freshman starting high school, he would get together about once a week with two other black students, Rik Smith, a junior, and Tony Peterson, a senior.

Peterson recalled that he and Barry discussed sports and religion and the social climate at Punahou, dwelling on which, if any, non-black girls would date black guys. "We talked about our classes and the charge that a black person with a book was acting white. We talked about the social issues of the day and whether we would see a black president in our lifetime. We discussed our vocational choices." He said the seeds of agony may have been there, but as a friend he did not sense Barry's inner turmoil.

Smith told reporters that Punahou could be a lonely place for an African-American in the '70s. "Those of us who were black did feel isolated," he told the *Associated Press*. Another black Punahou student, Lewis Anthony, Jr., explained that the "brothers" hung out together and went to parties at Schofield Barracks and other military bases, but he said he never saw Barry at the gatherings.

In his blistering 1995 memoir, the young Harvard Law School graduate described the missteps and milestones on his journey to being black in great detail. While he described his own thoughts and feelings unabashedly, he was wily in using pseudonyms and poetic license to fictionalize who his friends were and what they were telling him. *Chicago Tribune* columnist Lynn Sweet wrote that it was impossible to know who Obama's fellow students were because the characters in the book were not real people but "composites." Obama signaled in the book's introduction that he had made adjustments to his friends' personalities in order to protect their privacy. But the literary license also enabled him to give them words and ideas they never used.

The most memorable character in Obama's memoir of his Punahou years is the caustic, fast-talking Ray, who was two years ahead of him. Ray was a sadder but wiser student who brimmed with bitterness because blacks had to play on the white man's court by the white man's rules. In Ray's cosmology, it was a white-against-black, them-versus-us world, even though Barry reminded him that they were not living in Watts or Harlem or the Jim Crow South but in Hawai'i, where some of their best friends and basketball buddies were white, themselves ostracized from time to time by locals.

It was Ray who suggested that Barry wasn't getting as much playing time on the basketball courts on the Punahou team as he deserved because Barry was black. And it was Ray who told Barry that Punahou's *haole* and local girls were "USDA-certified racists" who would not go out with black guys, and that Asian girls were the most "racist" of all.

And it was Ray who offered to take Barry to parties at the university and on military bases where they could meet some "sisters" so that Barry could earn some points in the booty department.

Journalists who looked into Barry's past said the character of Ray, who felt most discriminated against because he was black, was based on Keith Kakugawa, a 1977 Punahou grad who was not black but *hapa*, being half-black and half-Japanese. Kakugawa told reporters that he never considered himself an outcast but was accepted, as were others who were *hapa*, or of mixed race. In interviews, Kakugawa said his conversations with Barry focused more on being left out of Punahou's moneyed elite than being racially excluded. They talked about assimilation and acceptance, he said. Kakugawa suggested that the feelings of isolation Barry expressed to him were more about being abandoned by his parents than being pigeonholed by racial discrimination in Hawai'i.

In fact, Barry seemed to have a much lower opinion of himself than anyone around him had of him. In the year that he burst onto the national scene with his DNC speech, Obama told the *Chicago Tribune* that had let his behavior slip in high school by "not focusing on my books" and "playing a lot of sports." He added that it wasn't until he left Hawai'i "that I started recognizing that I had bought into a set of false assumptions about what it means to be black."

In a 1999 note to his former school published in the Fall Punahou *Bulletin*, Obama put it more starkly: "My budding awareness of life's unfairness made for a more turbulent adolescence than perhaps some of my classmates experienced," he said. "As an African-American teenager with few African-Americans, I probably questioned my identity a bit harder than most. As a kid from a broken home and family of relatively modest means, I nursed more resentment than my circumstances justified, and didn't always channel those resentments in constructive ways."

But when news-gatherers descended on candidate Obama's 1979 classmates, they heard little of this. Instead, they mostly heard that Barry was well-liked and befriended by kids of all ethnic backgrounds.

Few if any saw the Barry who was tormented by interior struggle and searching for self-worth, in the words of Malcolm X. Despite all of the autobiographical anguish of the memoir, classmates recalled Barry as someone who was happy-go-lucky, fun to be with, well-motivated and well-adjusted enough to maintain a B average at a very demanding, nationally ranked prep school. They remembered him as the boy with the basketball and the smile, the jock who wrote poetry. His close friend Greg Orme said they spent time together at Gramps' place, listening to music on headphones, talking about all kinds of things, but not issues of race or isolation. "He was a very worldly, provocative speaker, but never about race," Orme told a reporter. Teammate Dan Hale recalled that Barry was a great communicator who found ways to relate to kids in the many cliques. The kid who could be tough on the basketball court could be gentle in the corridors. Kelli Furushima recalled that Barry playfully pulled a pencil off her ear as he passed her in a breezeway and signed her yearbook with a tender, self-effacing message about him being the one with his "Afro stickin' up again."

His teachers told news-gatherers that Barry behaved well and carried himself comfortably. If he was troubled by issues of racial identity, "he never let on," said high school homeroom teacher Eric Kusunoki. Kusunoki said Barry was "a normal kid like everyone else," but in a burst of pride when Obama announced his campaign for the presidency, Kusunoki said he was "a bright presence in the classroom."

Barry's old friends who talked to reporters said they had never really discussed race issues, but they did talk about drugs. In the late '70s, the influence of drugs was as pervasive at Punahou as it was on college campuses across the country. For many young people the terms "pop culture" and "drug culture" were merging. Barry's classmates say marijuana was cheap, and for that reason cocaine, which cost more, was considered higher class. Both were being used openly. Punahou students knew how to get drugs both on- and off-campus. One of the places they went to score pot or cocaine was the church just across the street from their high school math buildings. For some students, hallucinogenic and "hard" drugs were part of the Punahou party scene. Some turned on and tuned in to be accepted by a particular social group; others only experimented with drugs. At the same time, most students realized that they couldn't do drugs and perform all of the tasks Punahou expected of them.

While on the campaign trail in January 2008, Obama himself raised the subject of student drug use, as he had in his memoir, devoting half a page to his exploration of marijuana and at least one experience with cocaine. As he described it, the sensation of a match burning down to his fingertips reminded him of a time when he was so low he didn't care what happened to him. Toward the end of his time in Hawai'i, he had abandoned his letter-writing connection with his father. He was trying to blot out things about himself that he could not erase. "Pot had helped, and booze, [and] maybe a little blow when you could afford it," he recalled. He also described how a guy he knew who worked in a deli had ushered him into a meat freezer filled with salami to initiate him into the needle and tubing ritual of heroin use. But the thought that a bubble could end his life scared him. "Junkie. Pothead. That's where I'd been headed; the final, fatal role of the black man." Yet he said he was not experimenting with drugs to express solidarity with blacks; rather he was trying to block the reality of his identity out of his mind. These, he said in a campaign-trail talk to New Hampshire high school students, "were bad decisions." Barry's sister said her brother was not a serious drug user, merely a kid searching for answers.

Punahou School saw to it that Barry was challenged academically, although many of the challenges rolled off his back. Students in Barry's class of 1979 described a rigorously competitive curricular and extracurricular system that was designed to let students know where they stood in relation to classmates and teammates. They recall many kinds of measurements that focused attention on their competitive strengths and weaknesses versus those of their peers. They remember comparing how many gold, silver and bronze stars were put beside their names in early grades, which of their names were on team rosters and which were crossed off during tryouts for school teams, and which among them were singled out for awards and honors posted for all to see in the high school Administration Office. In retrospect, they say this constant competition and comparison was a real-world exercise that encouraged confidence among those who excelled in certain areas and discouraged others from pursuing fields in which they weren't among the best. This survival-of-the-fittest rivalry in middle school and high school prepared them for battles they would face getting into and getting ahead at highly competitive top-tier colleges. But Barry wasn't much interested in getting good grades and going to college. He would dash off an assignment the way he would take a quick basketball shot, just before the buzzer.

As a teenager, Barry was a rebel with a pause. After his hardheaded self had mastered the ability to win increasingly bitter arguments with Gramps, his softhearted self let his grandfather have his way, choosing to respect the *kupuna*, or elder, whose home he shared. While rebelling against the overall unfairness of things, Barry did a fair job of trying to be popular. Off the basketball court, he was putting his budding black personality and *Soul Train* style to work socially. Despite all the complaints about how black guys on campus couldn't get girls to go out with them, Barry had his share of friends, went to Punahou dances and had "the occasional awkward date."

The '70s were the heyday of teen social clubs in Hawai'i's high schools. Teen social clubs made it possible for the Isles' version of *American Bandstand* kids to break out of their small school groups and meet kids from other schools. Though they had bylaws and charters and came up with community service drives and talent shows, the most important mission of the teen clubs was to hold dance parties. In contrast to the squareness of their sponsors—the Hi-Y and Tri-Y of the YMCA and YWCA and Young Buddhist Association—the social clubs had fanciful names like those of doo-wop groups: the Assertions, Chevaliers, Crimson Joy, the Des Chandelles, Des Chanteys, Easy Riders, La Usherettes, the Mystic Sunlight, the Simple Pleasures, the Sheiks and the Tender Moments. There were parties every weekend at the Y or at a club member's house. With dozens of teen clubs at every Y, club members sometimes went to more than one dance on a Saturday night in order to meet boys or girls from other schools and get dates for the next event. At the height of the social phenomenon, club members carried teen club calling cards with names and numbers to hand out at parties and tack up on bulletin boards at participating merchants.

Punahou kids had no need to seek out the teen social clubs. Those from well-to-do families could hold get-togethers at their parents' country clubs, at the prestigious Outrigger Canoe Club on the shore by Diamond Head, or in spacious private homes. For the majority of students, after-school activity revolved around extra-curricular clubs and athletic teams at school, and there were veritably scores of options. Punahou's sheer size, not to mention its financial backing, made it possible to provide a rich variety of clubs and activities and the facilities to go with them. The after-school experience was an extension of the curriculum, designed to give students a chance to express themselves in a multitude of ways.

According to Punahou, Barry joined more than half a dozen clubs in the eight years he spent there. He was in Boys' Chorus in ninth grade and Concert Choir in 10th grade. In his senior year he contributed to the school's literary journal. He played on Punahou's middle school football team and junior varsity basketball team and spent his junior and senior years on the varsity basketball squad.

Barry was in charge of programming the pre-game music at basketball games, choosing rocking numbers by the Rolling Stones. His taste for jazz was a legacy from his father, which he shared with a few close friends, taking them to record stores to savor the sounds of George Benson, Grover Washington and other jazz artists. With other friends he was into the soul and R&B sounds of Marvin Gaye, Stevie Wonder and Earth Wind & Fire. In Hawai'i, as in the nation, Barry's last years in high school were infused with the disco beat, which had merged with the soul and R&B sounds of the '70s. The airwaves were filled with Fleetwood Mac, the Stones, the Bee Gees, the Commodores, the Doobie Brothers, Michael Jackson, Donna Summer and Gloria Gaynor. Yvonne Elliman and Better Midler, who went to high school in Hawai'i, also broke into the national charts during the Disco Era.

For most teenagers in Hawai'i, the '70s were was a time for rock music, experimenting with drugs, surfing and bodysurfing and cruising the beaches on weekends in search of good times, listening to eight-tracks on someone's car stereo. In Honolulu, as in bigger cities across the nation, disco was king when Barry entered his graduation year of 1979. *Grease, Saturday Night Fever* and *Star Wars* were big hits at the old Cinerama Theater that Barry would frequent with his friends.

After the movies and the basketball games, he and his teammates would head to Ward Warehouse, where they would dig in at Orson's Chowder House, or they would wind up at the Mister Burger Drive-In near the University of Hawai'i, for a burger or plate lunch. According to Bobby Titcomb, who was a year younger than Barry, the two of them sometimes liked to get away from it all by camping out overnight at the Peacock Flats camping area in the Mokulē'ia Forest Reserve, about as far from urban Honolulu as you can get on O'ahu.

At the start of his senior year, Barry had no real idea of what he would do after high school. In a conversation with his mother, who had returned from her field study in Indonesia, he postulated that a lot of life was about luck; you either caught some breaks or you didn't. It was only due to bad luck that one of his friends had been busted for possessing drugs, he said. In Hawai'i, Barry told his mother, if you were polite and didn't show too much attitude, you could get by unnoticed. When the time came to apply to colleges, Barry was thinking he could just hang out in Hawai'i and work part-time jobs. That rubbed his mother the wrong way, and she chided Barry for being too much into the good times and "too casual" about his future. Taking her point, he applied to Occidental College in Los Angeles because he had met a girl who lived near the Oxy campus.

At Punahou, every graduating senior submitted a quarter-page box for publication in the senior yearbook, *The Oahuan*. In his, Barry smiled out from a picture of himself wearing a short Afro and a disco shirt with a wide *Saturday Night Fever* collar, and with schoolboy bravado he thanked Toot, Gramps and the Choom Gang, a reference to his pot-smoking friends, "for all the good times." He also thanked a guy named Ray.

Barry graduated with 410 classmates in a commencement ceremony at the Neal Blaisdell Center. He sat next to Greg Orme, both young men handsome in dark sports coats and striped ties, the graduation uniform. The two friends were about to enter a new decade and an unknown future. By his own admission, Barry left Hawai'i for Los Angeles in 1979, angry and rebellious in the way many young black men are angry. It would be many years before he could look back at his Punahou years with a deep appreciation of the opportunity and experience it afforded him. In a *Sports Illustrated* interview, he paused to give props to his old school: "It is just an outstanding place to learn." ◌

CHAPTER TWELVE

"A RANGE OF DIFFERENT PEOPLE, CULTURES AND STYLES"
HAWAI'I'S MULTICULTURAL MILIEU

Like everyone who was born in Hawai'i, or chose to become part of Hawai'i, Barry interacted every day with people of the many ethnicities that had melted into local culture. Beyond the multiculturalism of his prep school campus, he remembered going to social occasions, which were always a hodgepodge of cultures, including the ubiquitous "potluck." Potlucks, and football-season tailgate parties, were typically multifamily eating events that included *pūpū*, or appetizers, and "plates" representative of Hawaiian, Chinese, Japanese, Portuguese, Korean and Filipino kitchens, in addition to other all-American fare.

Wherever he went on the island with Gramps or his classmates, "there would just be a range of different people, and you'd learn to appreciate people's different cultures and different styles."

For young Barry or anyone coming of age in Hawai'i, there may have been little conscious awareness that home was an island, a geographic speck among the most isolated inhabited group of islands on the face of the Earth. Life was a fairly constricted circuit of home, school, parties and playground, a summer job and home again. There was little time to think about isolation.

But growing up on an island cannot help but affect the way people see themselves in the world and in relation to other people, an approach that is materially different from the way people relate if they have come from the U.S. Mainland or any continental land mass. People who live on islands have an innate sense of interdependence and limits. Survival requires cooperation and mutual respect, traits that over time become ingrained and honored in the culture.

These are traits noticed by anthropologists among island people around the world. It is even a survival mechanism biologists have observed among plants and animals living on isolated islands. Cooperation and interdependence replace rugged individualism. The argument is that on a large land mass, when conflict arises or survival needs run short, a person can always move to the next state, the next frontier. That's not possible on islands.

Polynesian navigator Nainoa Thompson puts it in terms of a voyaging canoe: On islands, as on a canoe, we are all in it together, and survival depends on each of us pulling our weight cooperatively with one another. Island people have come to understand this, Thompson says, and as Earth becomes increasingly crowded, complicated and interconnected, the rest of the world is beginning to understand this as well. Earth becomes an island.

"When we look back at our history and our heritage," Thompson told a federal Ocean Policy Committee meeting in 2002, "there are very powerful lessons that tell us how these people learned in a very difficult way how to live well on islands, and I think that has become a philosophical global issue." On a day-to-day basis, this bedrock idea translates into a culture of modesty; acceptance, or at least tolerance, of others; and a willingness to share. You cannot have "red states" and "blue states" or their equivalent on an island. There isn't room for such divisions. The penalty for failure to cooperate is failure to survive.

Does this mean there's no conflict or cultural and racial tension on an island? Of course not. Hawai'i's story is peppered with shameful incidents of bigotry and conflict between races. None is more famous than the Massie Case, surely one of the most notorious criminal incidents in Hawai'i's history. In 1931, five Honolulu men, all of mixed local blood, were accused of the assault and rape of a white woman, Thalia Massie, based solely on her word and what turned out to be largely trumped-up evidence. When the five were let out on bail, Massie's Navy husband and her mother enlisted two men to kidnap one of the suspects. They shot him and attempted to hide the body. Massie's husband and the others, all of whom were white, were arrested, tried and convicted of manslaughter. Happily for them, they were then freed after just one hour in "prison" aboard a U.S. Navy ship at Pearl Harbor. Charges against the five local men were dropped for lack of evidence.

The topic of many books and movies, the Massie Case became the symbol of the race and class tensions that simmered beneath Hawai'i's benign surface in the pre-war years.

But the Massie "lynching" case was the exception rather than the rule in Hawai'i. The lesson learned, again and again, is that on an island, conflict poses a difficult choice. You cannot simply move away from conflict or tension and find a new place to settle. There are very real physical limits. Thus, it is best to find ways to work out an accommodation. Such lessons are not often explicitly taught in school or consciously passed down from generation to generation. But they become part of the culture and are felt by anyone living and growing within it. A well-worn pidgin phrase, familiar to any Hawai'i high school student, is the plantation-based admonition not to speak badly about someone else: "No talk stink."

As Barack Obama moved through Harvard Law School and politics, some of the people he encountered had a difficult time understanding his approach, an approach one might fairly call "Island style." One classmate from that famously competitive law school, reflecting what many Mainlanders perceive when encountering islanders, sounded a bit dismissive when he said he saw Obama as a little like Rodney King, writ large: "He just wants us all to get along."

But it's far more complex that that. Obama sought to explain this difficult concept during a mid-campaign interview with *U.S. News and World Report*:

"I do think that the multicultural nature of Hawai'i helped teach me how to appreciate different cultures and navigate different cultures, out of necessity," he said. "The second thing that I'm certain of is that what people often note as my even temperament I think draws from Hawai'i. People in Hawai'i generally don't spend a lot of time, you know, yelling and screamin' at each other. I think that there is just a cultural bias toward courtesy and trying to work through problems in a way that makes everybody feel like they're being listened to. And I think that reflects itself in my personality as well as my political style."

Inouye, the senior Hawai'i senator, put his own spin on what it is about islands that creates their own political and social culture. "There is a border called the ocean," he said. "You can't move to the suburbs and live in a mansion. You find it necessary to live with each other."

By his senior year, Barry, who had arrived at Punahou as a chubby, awkward 10-year-old, had been transformed into a tall, good-looking basketball player with a killer smile. A yearbook photo shows Obama with a group of classmates in full disco mode: sharp white jacket, wide-collared shirt and carefully trimmed Afro.

His yearbook captured the focus and fascination of his classmates at the time: surfing, the beach, parties and youthful optimism combined with painful naiveté. At one costume party (who knows if Barry was there), three of his classmates were a big hit as "plantation slaves" in black face, corn-rowed hair and overalls. The slaves costume that Halloween was not a big hit with the handful of black students, who never forgot it.

Like many people at that time, some of Obama's Hawaiian classmates began listening to their elders, the wise *kūpuna* who held on to cultural knowledge until the next generation was ready to embrace it. The need to understand and appreciate the Hawaiian culture was felt by students of every race and ethnicity.

As he has written, Obama was on a similar, but in many ways quite different, journey. Obama wanted to discover and understand his own unique identity, that of a young black American. All around him, young people in the Islands were discovering their own roots and their own identities. To be Hawaiian or Japanese or Filipino—or, increasingly in mixed-race Hawai'i, to be *hapa*—was a matter of newfound pride.

It had to be a powerful lesson.

But what if you weren't one of the races that made up the Hawaiian "stew"? What if you were seen by the rest of the world as black? What sense would it make to take *hula* lessons, attend Japanese *bon* dances or learn, as so many young people did then, how to play popular Hawaiian songs on the guitar? If you were a young man identified as black, where did your search for cultural and ethnic roots take you then?

Through his grandmother and grandfather, Barry understood his white, mid-American Kansas roots and values. He speaks about those roots with pride to this day. What he didn't know, or understand, is what it meant to be a black man in America. As he has written, that question drove him to seek out African-American friends, to read black literature and to adopt a black persona.

The search also took this questioning young high school student to an unlikely place: the bohemian backwaters of Waikīkī. By the mid-'70s, big hotels lined the beach and sunburned visitors thronged on Kalākaua Avenue. But the resort area had yet to go through the complete and massive redevelopment that shaped what it is today. In those days, just blocks away from the hotels and high-rise condominiums, much of the old Waikīkī Jungle remained.

The "jungle" was a collection of tiny lanes, flimsy shacks, unimposing concrete walk-up apartments and shady backyards where rents were cheap and times were good. It was a haven for surfers, beach bums and folks down on their luck. At night, it was raucous with the sound of drinking parties and backyard barbecues.

As a high school student, long after he had stopped going around with Gramps as his guide, Barry would drive Gramps' Ford to this rundown part of Waikīkī. There he would have heart-to-heart conversations with his grandpa's drinking buddy, Frank Marshall Davis. Barry remembered that when Gramps had first introduced them, he had thought of Davis as an old man "with a big dewlapped face and an ill-kempt Afro that made him look like an old, shaggy-maned lion." By the time Barry was old enough to drive, the octogenarian had become a friend and in many ways a cultural mentor. Davis was separated from his wife and children. He had moved into a small bungalow in the Waikiki Jungle, where he conducted a continuing "salon" for drinkers, dreamers, the intellectually curious and others. Seated in a green armchair, with jazz from his enormous collection of 78s on the record player, a television blaring in the background and a pot of greens or sweet potatoes for pie simmering on the stove, Davis would entertain anyone who chose to drop by. For Barry, who visited him right up until the time he left Hawai'i, Davis was the *kupuna* who held cultural knowledge similar to that which young Hawaiians were rediscovering elsewhere.

Barry might not have known at first that his grandpa's buddy had been a well-known journalist, labor activist, poet and writer who had a unique perspective on what it is like to be black in America and, more specifically, black in Hawai'i. Davis had achieved prominence in Chicago for his writing and work as an editor with the *Associated Negro Press* and, earlier, as editor of one of the nation's first successful black newspapers. Already a published poet, Davis traveled to Hawai'i in 1948 with his wife, white Chicago socialite Helen Canfield Davis, ostensibly on a temporary writing assignment, and ended up living there the rest of his life. He was lionized by Honolulu society when he first arrived but soon fell out of favor, in large part due to his association with the leftist International Longshoremen's and Warehousemen's Union, a tough, no-nonsense union that at the time was furiously organizing Hawai'i's plantations and docks. The year after Davis arrived, the ILWU organized a massive strike against the territory's dominant business interests, primarily over the issue of wage parity between Hawai'i workers and union members on the West Coast.

That painful 1949 dock strike signaled the emergence of the union and its members, mostly Asian and of immigrant stock, as a political power to be reckoned with. It was also a power to be feared. The union and those who ran with it were soon targets of suspicion and legal harassment as McCarthyism and the Red Scare heated up. By all accounts, Davis insisted he was not a card-carrying Communist, but his association with the union certainly gave him that reputation. In the eyes of the people who ran things (and apparently the FBI as well), "I was a Communist and a subversive and a threat to Hawai'i," Davis once ruefully recalled.

Kathryn Waddell Takara, a professor at the University of Hawai'i, has written extensively about Davis and his time in Hawai'i and his unusual perspective on race and ethnic relations in the Islands.

"Blacks in Hawai'i had a certain fluidity between several ethnic groups which afforded Davis a unique platform from which to observe and discuss the consequences of the new (Hawaiian) economy," she wrote in a paper titled "Frank Marshall Davis—Black Labor Activist and Outsider Journalist: Social Movements in Hawai'i."

"He wrote of the parallels of laws and influences between the Southern plantation system and plantations in Hawai'i, as well as parallels between Blacks and Hawaiians," Takara wrote. "His insight into colonial techniques and strategies for dividing the minorities/oppressed groups, his ability to see beyond the binary racism so common in the continental U.S. and his documentation of discrimination and racism in Hawai'i are testament to Davis's role as a significant voice and witness in the historical process of Hawai'i's economic development, inter-group relationships and changing social consciousness."

Davis was convinced that coalition politics was the best way for oppressed groups to achieve justice and equality. That surely was a lesson learned by Hawai'i's Filipino, Japanese and other ethnic plantation workers, who set aside ethnic and racial suspicions to work together in their struggles against the iron rule of the plantation owners. The coalitions forged in those early labor struggles formed the backbone of the Democratic Party's rise to power, a power that lasted for more than four decades and was at its peak when Barry was in high school.

Davis would regularly read from his poetry for his guests. One of those poems, "This is Paradise," captures the role of the ILWU and the unions in Hawai'i's modern history in this excerpt:

"The devil doesn't ask shorter hours, higher pay
Like Harry Bridges and his ILWU
Men on the wide plantations
Those handling cargo on the waterfront
Hung hang-me-down hates in the closet
And organized
In one big union
Japanese, Chinese, Filipino, Portuguese, Puerto Rican, Hawaiian, Korean
And together
Raised their voices for a living share of the take

And treatment as men and women
The Big Five sneered
Flexed its muscles
And hit—
But the Union stood and fought
Growing strong in struggle
Then the onlookers
Seeing the Big Five no longer king
Themselves grew bold
Forming their own corporations
Biting the sweet apple of independence—"

"People saw him as a father figure," said Takara. "He talked a lot about organizing and social justice. I'm sure [Barry] was hearing that. He was a big, strong, articulate principled man who had accomplished much in his life." Takara says she hears echoes of Davis in Obama's rhetoric. "He really wanted America to come up to what it was supposed to be," she said. "He loved democracy. Change and hope: He embodied both of those things in all his writings."

Whether or not the youngster Barry Obama learned these lessons of coalition politics at Davis's knee, he certainly came to practice them when he arrived in Chicago and plunged into the difficult work of political organizing in Chicago's tough neighborhoods. Along with the limericks and reminiscing Stanley Dunham and Frank Davis enjoyed so much, was there talk during those long Waikīkī nights of labor's hope for a more just and equitable society? Was young Barry listening?

Davis had come to Hawai'i from Chicago in search of a place where he could escape the racial tension that plagued him at home and where he could see his dream of coalition politics and the power of organized labor played out on a new and still untested field. Obama would eventually reverse this journey, leaving the beaches and easy friendships of Hawai'i behind to find his way to Chicago, where he would explore his own racial identity and work to build bridges where far too few existed.

For all his geniality and close friendships with whites, Davis was also angry, an anger he shared with Barry. Davis had come to realize that his status in territorial and post-territorial Hawai'i had more to do with the fact that, while he was not white, he was also not "Oriental." He bridged a huge cultural gulf in the Islands.

In a column written in 1950, long before those whiskey nights in the Waikīkī Jungle, Davis began to put shape to his anger and concerns about colonialism and imperialism in a column in the ILWU newspaper, the *Honolulu Record*.

"To the people of Hawai'i: Africa is a far-away place, almost another world," he wrote. "And yet in many ways it is as close as your next-door neighbor. The Dark Continent suffers from a severe case of the disease known as colonialism, which Hawai'i has in a much milder form. The sole hope of the dying empires of Western Europe is intensified exploitation and continued slavery of African workers through U.S. money and munitions. There are strikes in Africa against the same kinds of conditions that cause strikes in Hawai'i.

"Maybe you think of Africans as black savages, half-naked, dancing to the thump-thump of tom-toms in jungle clearings, if you think of it at all. You may have gotten your impressions through the propaganda of press, radio and films, intended to sell the world on the idea that Africans are inferior and backward.

"It comes from the same propaganda mill," he wrote, "that sells Mainlanders the idea that Japanese and Chinese and Filipinos and other people of different cultures and colors are also inferior and backward."

As an ardent friend of labor, Davis became close to left-leaning labor organizers in the Islands, including the ILWU giant Harry Bridges and his man in Hawai'i, Jack Hall. While Davis and the ILWU radicals suffered during the red-baiting days of the 1950s, the union leaders would eventually come to be recognized and honored in Hawai'i as central players in the state's economic success and in the rise of the Japanese, Filipino and other plantation classes into full participation in the Hawaiian dream. In the history of the Islands, Hall and those who worked alongside him, like Davis, became authentic working-class heroes. Their union and the multicultural workers it represented fought for and won a seat at the table for Hawai'i's working-class men and women.

One has to wonder what Davis would think today if he could watch his old labor friends memorialized as heroic builders of today's successful multiethnic Hawai'i and his buddy's questioning grandson grow into the man who would accept the nomination of his party to run for president of the United States.

While Davis was understandably cynical about the future of race and ethnic relations in Hawai'i as well as in the rest of the United States, he remained hopeful, if not entirely optimistic, that Hawai'i could teach something to the rest of the world. He concluded one of a series of articles on race relations with these words: "These beautiful islands can still chart their own future." And in a 1949 article in a publication named *The Crisis*, which was aimed at black Americans on the Mainland, Davis had kind words for Hawai'i. "If you have no need for the black ghetto, if you like an even climate averaging 71 degrees in winter and 76 in summer, coral beaches and mountains, leisurely living, beautiful scenery and beautiful people, Hawai'i is what you always dreamed about," he wrote. "And, along with these things, you also get the closest approach to real democracy available anywhere under the Stars and Stripes."

But as Obama remembered it, that optimism was tempered by the reality of what it means to be a black person in Hawai'i and in America today.

At one point, Davis and Barry were discussing an incident in which Barry's grandmother was frightened by a street person at a bus stop—a black person, as it turned out. Her husband had argued there was no reason to be afraid. It was an incident Obama recalled again during the presidential campaign when he gave his seminal speech on race relations.

Here's how Obama remembered that moment, sitting and listening to Davis in the humid Honolulu night: "'What I'm trying to tell you is, your grandma's right to be scared,'" Obama recalled Davis saying. "'She's at least as right as Stanley is. She understands that black people have a reason to hate. That's just how it is. For your sake, I wish it were otherwise. But it's not. So you might as well get used to it.'"

"I knew for the first time," Obama reported, "that I was utterly alone." One imagines that Barry walked out of Frank Davis's house that night feeling like a stranger in paradise. ⁂

CHAPTER THIRTEEN

"The values I hold dear"
The Lessons of Hawai'i

It would be 12 years between Barry Obama's 1979 high school graduation in Hawai'i and Barack Hussein Obama's 1991 graduation from Harvard Law School. In the intervening years, he had started his undergraduate college education at Occidental College in Los Angeles and completed it at New York's Columbia University, where he had majored in political science and focused on international affairs. By 1982, he had dropped the nickname Barry and his lackadaisical attitude toward academic achievement and entered a new, longer-lasting life phase as an overachiever. He moved to Chicago in 1985 to become a community organizer. Inspired by dreams from his mother, he began working with a church group to help people of all colors and creeds escape the plight of poverty, unemployment and discrimination.

After three years of work as a community organizer in low-income neighborhoods of Chicago, Obama made his first trip to Kenya. In 1988, he began his postgraduate studies at Harvard, the same university his father had abandoned him for, and went on to earn a law degree and the distinction of becoming the first African-American president of the *Harvard Law Review*, in large part because his classmates said he was a coalition builder, someone who could bridge the political gulf between liberal and conservative students. The law students were experiencing an Island-style approach.

Settling into a prestigious Chicago firm, Barack Obama practiced civil rights law and taught constitutional law, and wooed and won as his bride Michelle Robinson, a lawyer from the firm. They had two daughters and became actively involved in their Christian faith. Finally, Obama's calling for public service motivated him to run for elective office. He won a seat in the Illinois State Senate, which he held for eight years, and lost a bid for election to Congress.

Barack Obama's stepfather, Lolo Soetoro, died in 1987 of a liver ailment. Maya recalled in interviews that after her parents passed away, older brother Barack stepped up his interest in her. They had a lot in common. They lived together for a time in Chicago. They talked about poetry and philosophy, took long walks, enjoyed listening to jazz. She recalled that the first book he gave her was by noted African-American author Toni Morrison, who would later endorse Barack Obama for president. It was he who took her on a trip to look at colleges. It was he who opened her eyes to all the possibilities the world has to offer people who embrace all the options. And it was he who taught her to cook the three dishes he knew. One of them was chili, which he cooked for his family one Christmas when they couldn't get reservations at a restaurant. "He was a great big brother," she said, "who stepped into a parenting role offering guidance on self-respect, pride and, Hawaiian style, humility."

Gramps, who had introduced Barry to Hawai'i's charms, died in 1992 and was buried with military honors at the National Memorial Cemetery of the Pacific, Punchbowl, the iconic volcanic crater that overlooked his Honolulu apartment.

Obama's mother, Stanley Ann Dunham, died of ovarian and uterine cancer in November 1995, shortly after publication of her son's groundbreaking first book. Although she had been sick, his mother's death at age 52 caught Obama by surprise. Had he known, he might have written a very different first book, focusing on the woman he would later describe as "the most positive influence in my life." He dedicated his second book, *The Audacity of Hope*, to her and to Toot, "the women who raised me." He called his *tūtū* "a rock of stability throughout his life," and of his mother, a decade after her passing, he said, "her loving spirit sustains me still."

Obama and his sister scattered their mother's ashes at sea from a rocky point near Sandy Beach. Back in Washington, he hung a picture on the wall of his U.S. Senate office to remind him of his mom and Hawai'i, his boyhood home. It was a picture of crashing surf at the place where he had scattered her remains.

His mother would have been especially proud of him on July 27, 2004, when he gave that Democratic National Convention speech that brought him to the world's attention.

Although he talked about his dream of an America that was not divided by race, class or creed, a nation that celebrated and embraced its diversity, Barack Obama did not say much about Hawai'i in that now-famous speech. In fact, most of what Obama did say about the Islands was not even included in the prepared text. His "narrative," and indeed that of the convention as a whole, required Obama to focus on his work in Chicago, building communities and building bridges between races, political factions and generations.

But it seemed to many gathered around their television sets back in the Islands that Obama was in fact talking about Hawai'i. Obama's dream for America was already within reach, if not fully realized, in Hawai'i.

Pick up a Sunday newspaper in Honolulu on any weekend and page through the splashy ads for new housing subdivisions, furniture or any of the dream goods of the perfect American life. Look carefully at the handsome young couple pictured enjoying their new home or their newly enhanced lifestyle. The couple is almost surely multiracial, he perhaps Caucasian and she perhaps Asian or Hawaiian. If there are kids in the picture, they are a happy blend of the two. The marketing experts who produce these ads know what they are doing. They are picturing the ideal demographic for Hawai'i. It is a demographic that does more than sell furniture. It also sells political ideals. And Obama may have been thinking about that when he talked about a more perfect America.

Ethnicity is an important part of politics in Hawai'i. But it plays out in ways unfamiliar to most people on the Mainland. On much of the Mainland, ethnic politics is a matter of clan affiliation at its most benign (Irish vote for Irish; Poles vote for Poles), while it can also manifest as something far darker: class resentment, distrust, even outright hostility or racism.

Throughout his career in New York, Chicago and Washington, Hawai'i remained a constant for Barack Obama. From 1982 through 2006, he visited Hawai'i virtually every year to see his *tūtū*. He would also take his family to the beach, to look for sea turtles, to run around in Kapi'olani Park and to eat shave-ice. He would take pleasure in pigging out on fresh *sashimi*, and its Island-style variation, *poke*, which is cubed and seasoned raw fish; and maybe get in some basketball, golf and beach time at Sandys with his high school buddies. But Christmas 2007 came and went without a visit. Urgent business prevented him from visiting the state where he was born.

In a December 2007 telephone interview with Honolulu's most popular radio personalities, Michael W. Perry and Larry Price, Obama tried to cement his credentials as a "local boy." Perry and Price quickly dismissed political questions and got to the meat of the matter, the Local Quiz. Which would he choose? they asked:

Zippy's chili or Zippy's version of saimin, Zipmin?
Answer: Zipmin.
Shave-ice or SPAM musubi?
Answer: Shave-ice.

"Hawaiian Moving Company" (Perry's popular local TV show) or Oprah?
"I gotta go with Oprah," Obama admitted.

The popular radio duo pressed Obama on whether, if elected, he would make Hawai'i the Vacation White House similar to Ronald Reagan's Western White House and George Bush's Texas White House. Obama was careful with his answer.

"You know," he said, "this is the first Christmas where I haven't been back in Hawai'i for the entire 25 years I have been on the Mainland. You know what that means? I want to come back to Hawai'i every year. It's still a big part of me. Some of my best friends are still living on the island. It's definitely going to be a priority if I can get some time off," he said.

If he now found himself prodigiously pressed for time to visit, it was due to something that had happened during that last trip, for the 2006 holiday season, something that made it impossible for Obama to return the following Christmas. It was in Hawai'i, surrounded by his family, that Obama had made the final decision to run for president.

During the 2008 Democratic primaries, there were startling exit poll results that made it clear many Americans still base their vote on race, and race alone. Across many states, a surprising number of white voters told pollsters they would never vote for a black man. Even after Obama had proven his viability by winning the Democratic nomination against a slate of formidable opponents led by Senator Clinton, the voters had doubts.

Now, it would be easy to dismiss this as simple racism. But it is more likely a statement that some voters do not believe a black person could ever fully understand or empathize with them and their problems and concerns. This may be true in the world of politics, but it's truly strange in light of the fact that the two most influential and wealthiest figures in America's billion-dollar entertainment and sports world are Oprah Winfrey and Tiger Woods.

By the same token, Obama received overwhelming support from African-American voters during the primaries. Correctly or incorrectly, they assumed that a candidate with Obama's face would instinctively understand their political needs and wants. It made perfect sense to support him. But if Obama teaches any lesson about all this from the Hawai'i perspective, it is that it is possible to get beyond simple ethnic analysis and into something far more complex and, well, more interesting. Ethnicity plays an important, but quite subtle, role in Hawai'i politics. It is not too much to say that Hawai'i's approach to ethnic politics will one day soon become the nation's approach. Barack Obama's candidacy is helping to hasten that day.

In the early '70s, the then-lieutenant governor commissioned a study on the demographics of voting in Hawai'i. The official purpose of the study was to develop a database that would be useful in producing a fair electoral reapportionment. But the other interest was pure curiosity: How does ethnic voting play out in a multiethnic, fully diverse society?

The answer was clear. Yes, people tend to cluster their votes around candidates of their same ethnic background—when everything else is equal. In the enduring words of the study, ethnicity is important in Hawai'i elections, "but ethnicity is not destiny." Indeed, as Hawai'i matures and becomes more multiracial, closer to the fictional "Golden People" imagined in James Michener's *Hawaii*, the less race seems to matter in elective politics in Obama's home state.

A more recent study of the demographic patterns of voting in Hawai'i by the *Honolulu Advertiser* after the 2000 elections underscored what the lieutenant governor's office learned 30 years previously: Yes, voters tend to drift to candidates who share their ethnicity. Caucasians do well among Caucasian voters, Hawaiian candidates score heavily among voters who consider themselves Hawaiian.

If an ambitious young man or woman wants to run for office from heavily Hawaiian areas along O'ahu's Leeward Coast, it helps if the candidate can talk about his or her family's Hawaiian roots. In blue-collar Kalihi, where many newly arrived Filipino immigrants live, it is obviously an advantage to be of Filipino extraction. And candidates of mixed race or with names that do not reveal their ethnicity are careful to include their ethnic identifier name on the ballot: Patsy Takemoto Mink or Jean Sadako King or, as one unfortunate and eventually unsuccessful Caucasian candidate named himself: "John Aloha Mahalo Fritz."

But the most controlling demographic factor in Hawai'i elections, at least today, is not ethnicity, nor is it gender, nor is it age. It is income. There is more bloc voting in Hawai'i among people of similar income groups than there is for any other demographic. In other words, affluent people find themselves sharing political interests and candidates with others with wealth. Similarly, Hawai'i voters of limited means tend to vote like others in the same income bracket, no matter what their ethnicity or gender.

Voting according to one's pocketbook is nothing new, in Hawai'i or anywhere else. But the fact that income or pocketbook issues trump ethnicity in the Islands allows Hawai'i to teach the world a complex lesson about ethnic politics. Cut open any politician in Hawai'i and you will find someone analyzing potential votes on the basis of race and ethnicity. But race is usually a shorthand for a more complex analysis: class, union membership, geographic distribution and, as always, income.

In Hawai'i today, the best ethnic identity a candidate can have is *hapa*, a person blended from the many races that make the state what it is. Beyond his self-identification as a black man, could it be that Barack Obama is our first true national *hapa* candidate?

As he himself would suggest, who else could bring change to the White House better than a president who has African relatives living on the shores of Lake Victoria, a white grandmother living in a Honolulu high-rise, and a sister who is half-Indonesian and married to a Chinese-Canadian? ∝

CHAPTER FOURTEEN

"IF YOU'RE ON A WAVE, YOU RIDE IT"
THE CAMPAIGN SEEN FROM HAWAI'I

Hawai'i's Democratic Party caucus meetings in February 2008 were not expected to mean much of anything in the epic national battle to determine who would win the party's presidential nomination. By mid-February, the thinking went, the race would be all but settled on the Mainland. And indeed that had been the case in past years, when only the committed or terminally bored bothered to show up for precinct caucuses. These were sleepy exercises in school cafeterias and meeting rooms where party regulars took turns electing themselves to various offices and casting largely symbolic votes for presidential candidates.

On the morning of February 19, party leaders were anxious. They were concerned about the weather. Would predictions of light rain discourage people from showing up? They fretted about logistics. Anticipating a surge of interest, they doubled supplies and recruited more volunteer workers when they heard that 10,000 or even 12,000 people might participate.

Young volunteers with new energy worked the phones in a bid to interest voters in the Hawai'i-born candidate. Hawai'i's KITV reported that when a volunteer dialed a Madelyn Dunham to ask for her vote, Barry's *tūtū* said: "Honey, you don't have to convince me. Barack Obama is my grandson."

As it turned out, no amount of planning or worrying could have anticipated what happened that day. In an explosion of political interest never before seen in the Islands, more than 37,000 people turned out to participate in this most American demonstration of grassroots participatory democracy. Thirty-seven thousand people! On a Monday work night. That's a staggering number for an event that on a good year barely drew 5,000 people. The vast majority of those who found caucus sites, from remote Na'alehu on the Big Island to crowded school sites in urban Honolulu supported Obama. After a state convention settled additional delegate slots, Obama won 21 Hawai'i votes at the national Democratic convention to Hillary Clinton's eight. The last delegate added was retired Judge James Burns, the son and near look-alike of the late governor who had led Hawai'i's polyglot Democrats to political power four long decades earlier. Burns, who knew Obama and his family, said he was asked personally by the candidate to stand as a delegate, a fitting and symbolic choice in Hawai'i.

"We saw history being made tonight," cried an exultant Congressman Abercrombie, Obama's most visible political cheerleader in the state. Traffic backed up for blocks around caucus sites. Good-natured lines of eager voters—many, as it turned out, brand-new to the party and this political process—waited for hours to get in and get registered. Precinct officials quickly ran out of ballots and voter registration forms. What was supposed to be an orderly process soon turned into semi-chaos, with people scribbling their votes on scraps of paper and promising to register as voters and party members as soon as they could. It was a meltdown but, for most who participated, a happy meltdown.

In Mānoa, not far from where Barry Obama lived as a child, the numbers overwhelmed any sense of order. Standing on a table, Abercrombie shouted through a bullhorn that because of the turnout, the rules would be scrapped and from then on everyone would be "on the honor system." Never mind that the rules made no provision for an honor system. Everyone knew what was happening and why the crowds were there: Entranced, mesmerized, stirred by a presidential candidate as they had not been in two generations, people were willing to play by any rules just so they could say, on this night, "I voted for Barack Obama, who was born and bred in Hawai'i." An astonishing number of people were not just new to the Democratic Party; they were new to voting as well.

Of course, the old-timers who usually dominate and run such events were on hand as well. So, too, was a much smaller but determined band of Hillary Clinton supporters. But most of the crowd, many in casual shorts, T-shirts and aloha wear, had little interest in electing precinct officers or dealing with other matters of routine party business. They had one goal in mind: to cast a vote in the straw poll for Barack Obama.

Hawai'i has had its spasms of political excitement before. But never anything like this. In the past, experienced political leaders and their patient, loyal followers would find a way to outsmart and outwork enthusiastic but inexperienced newcomers. For a while, it looked as if the same pattern would repeat itself this time around. Yes, Obama would do well—after all, he was a hometown hero of sorts, wasn't he? But the Clinton forces had the institutional support of the state's well-organized unions and the backing of big-clout political leaders such as the widely respected Inouye, Hawai'i's senior senator, and State Senate President Colleen Hanabusa. Would they find a way to prevail?

Unfortunately for Clinton, Obama proved to be a different kind of candidate, a candidate who was shattering assumptions not just on the Mainland but in Hawai'i as well. In an unguarded moment, Inouye let slip a thought that revealed just how far the political ground had shifted in the Islands.

Asked by a *Honolulu Advertiser* reporter whether he felt Obama deserved support in Hawai'i because he was from the Islands, Inouye said this:

"If you ask the people in Hawai'i what they know about Barack Obama, I think the honest answer is, 'very little,'" Inouye said. "He went to school in Hawai'i, but he went to Punahou, and that was not a school for the impoverished.

"I don't hold it against anyone who is a Punahou grad. It's a fine school. I would say one of the finest in the United States. But to suggest that Punahou maybe set his life plan in place, I find it very interesting," said Inouye, a 1942 graduate of the public McKinley High School.

While many who grew up in Hawai'i understood Inouye's unstated point about the perceived isolation of the Punahou world, the public backlash was immediate—and generally negative.

Coming from one of the U.S. Senate's oldest and most respected members, who had championed Hawai'i causes in Washington since Statehood, the Punahou-bashing remark caused a wave of protest from Obama supporters and Punahou alumni. Some noted that Inouye had overlooked the fact that granting scholarships had enabled Punahou to provide a rich cultural experience in an environment of ethnic and socioeconomic diversity.

"Excuse me, Senator Inouye?" said Alana Lambert Bryan, who suggested that Inouye hadn't done his homework. "When was the last time you looked over the financial situation of Punahou students' families?" she asked him, in a letter to the editor. "There are hundreds of students who rely on Punahou's financial aid, and parents who work two jobs to give them the best education possible."

Katie Graham, a college teacher in Oakland, California, advised Inouye to check Punahou's Web site, which states: "Punahou maintains a long-standing commitment to provide need-based financial aid. A family's financial status does not influence admission decisions."

Punahou alumna Toni Auld Yardley, a Native Hawaiian activist, reminded Inouye: "The roots of Punahou are as strong as the *lauhala* tree and water spring upon which it was built and [which] is its emblem."

Speaking of his Senate colleague, 37 years his senior, Obama said sharply: "Shame on Danny for trying that stunt." Obama told a television station. "I went to Punahou on a scholarship. I was raised by a single mom and my grandmother. I know the people of Hawai'i. I know the problems of Hawai'i. I know the opportunities of Hawai'i. And the culture is my culture. I learned very early on in Hawai'i how to bring people together, all the different cultures and that spirit of aloha that's so important," he said.

He campaigned via news media, via satellite, telling one TV interviewer: "As someone who grew up there and understands the people, who cares deeply about the state, I think the people of Hawai'i can count on having a president who is thinking about them." He told Hawai'i's KGMB-TV: "I am looking forward to being the first Hawaiian-born president in the White House."

After years of struggling to find his place in the world, Obama was able to say he knew where his home was and where, perhaps, his heart truly belonged.

And on that night at least, as the Hawaiian skies darkened and thousands of people, young and old, of every race and background, waited patiently through the evening to cast their one ballot, Barack "Barry" Obama was anything but alone.

Then, four months later, on the night of June 3, 2008, a historic, exhausting and emotionally draining primary campaign was finally over. Obama had accumulated enough convention delegate votes to secure a victory over a formidable and tradition-shattering candidate in her own right, Hillary Clinton. Before an adoring crowd of thousands in St. Paul's Xcel Center, the very site Republicans would use for their national convention later that year, Obama took time to thank the many who had brought him that far. Above all of them: Madelyn Payne Dunham, his *haole tūtū*.

"Thank you to my grandmother, who helped raise me and is sitting in Hawai'i somewhere right now because she can't travel but who poured everything she had into me, who helped make me the man I am today. Tonight is for her," Obama declared.

In Honolulu, now largely confined to her apartment due to age and osteoporosis, Toot was watching. She heard her grandson throw his thoughts, however briefly, back to Hawai'i. "She was extremely proud and rather overwhelmed," Maya remembered. "She just kept saying, 'Oh my, oh my.' She was incredibly touched."

The candidate was still on stage when his grandmother dialed his number to leave a message that she was proud and that she loved him. "Did she cry?" his sister was asked. "No," Soetoero-Ng said. "She's not the crying type."

The next day, two Hawai'i state Department of Health social workers were gushing about Obama. One of the social workers was born in the Philippines and raised in Hawai'i. The other was born in Kenya and educated in Hawai'i. Both were moved by Obama's impassioned oratory and the universality of the themes and values he espoused.

"That's his Hawaiianness," said the one raised in Hawai'i. "That's his Kenyanness," said the other. ෆ

2004 DEMOCRATIC NATIONAL CONVENTION
KEYNOTE ADDRESS

Thank you so much. Thank you. Thank you. Thank you so much. Thank you so much. Thank you. Thank you. Thank you, Dick Durbin. You make us all proud.

On behalf of the great state of Illinois, crossroads of a nation, Land of Lincoln, let me express my deepest gratitude for the privilege of addressing this convention.

Tonight is a particular honor for me because, let's face it, my presence on this stage is pretty unlikely. My father was a foreign student, born and raised in a small village in Kenya. He grew up herding goats, went to school in a tin-roof shack. His father—my grandfather—was a cook, a domestic servant to the British.

But my grandfather had larger dreams for his son. Through hard work and perseverance my father got a scholarship to study in a magical place, America, that shone as a beacon of freedom and opportunity to so many who had come before.

While studying here, my father met my mother. She was born in a town on the other side of the world, in Kansas. Her father worked on oil rigs and farms through most of the Depression. The day after Pearl Harbor my grandfather signed up for duty; joined Patton's army, marched across Europe. Back home, my grandmother raised a baby and went to work on a bomber assembly line. After the war, they studied on the G.I. Bill, bought a house through F.H.A., and later moved west all the way to Hawai'i in search of opportunity.

And they, too, had big dreams for their daughter. A common dream, born of two continents.

My parents shared not only an improbable love, they shared an abiding faith in the possibilities of this nation. They would give me an African name, Barack, or "blessed," believing that in a tolerant America your name is no barrier to success. They imagined—They imagined me going to the best schools in the land, even though they weren't rich, because in a generous America you don't have to be rich to achieve your potential.

They're both passed away now. And yet, I know that on this night they look down on me with great pride.

They stand here—And I stand here today, grateful for the diversity of my heritage, aware that my parents' dreams live on in my two precious daughters. I stand here knowing that my story is part of the larger American story, that I owe a debt to all of those who came before me, and that, in no other country on earth, is my story even possible.

Tonight, we gather to affirm the greatness of our Nation—not because of the height of our skyscrapers, or the power of our military, or the size of our economy. Our pride is based on a very simple premise, summed up in a declaration made over two hundred years ago:

> We hold these truths to be self-evident, that all men are created equal,
> that they are endowed by their Creator with certain inalienable rights,
> that among these are Life, Liberty and the pursuit of Happiness.

That is the true genius of America, a faith—a faith in simple dreams, an insistence on small miracles; that we can tuck in our children at night and know that they are fed and clothed and safe from harm; that we can say what we think, write what we think, without hearing a sudden knock on the door; that we can have an idea and start our own business without paying a bribe; that we can participate in the political process without fear of retribution, and that our votes will be counted—at least most of the time.

This year, in this election we are called to reaffirm our values and our commitments, to hold them against a hard reality and see how we're measuring up to the legacy of our forbearers and the promise of future generations.

And fellow Americans, Democrats, Republicans, Independents, I say to you tonight: We have more work to do—more work to do for the workers I met in Galesburg, Illinois, who are losing their union jobs at the Maytag plant that's moving to Mexico, and now are having to compete with their own children for jobs that pay seven bucks an hour; more to do for the father that I met who was losing his job and choking back the tears, wondering how he would pay $4500 a month for the drugs his son needs without the health benefits that he counted on; more to do for the young woman in East St. Louis, and thousands more like her, who has the grades, has the drive, has the will, but doesn't have the money to go to college.

Now, don't get me wrong. The people I meet—in small towns and big cities, in diners and office parks—they don't expect government to solve all their problems. They know they have to work hard to get ahead, and they want to. Go into the collar counties around Chicago, and people will tell you they don't want their tax money wasted, by a welfare agency or by the Pentagon. Go in—Go into any inner city neighborhood, and folks will tell you that government alone can't teach our kids to learn; they know that parents have to teach, that children can't achieve unless we raise their expectations and turn off the television sets and eradicate the slander that says a black youth with a book is acting white. They know those things.

People don't expect—People don't expect government to solve all their problems. But they sense, deep in their bones, that with just a slight change in priorities, we can make sure that every child in America has a decent shot at life, and that the doors of opportunity remain open to all.

They know we can do better. And they want that choice.

In this election, we offer that choice. Our Party has chosen a man to lead us who embodies the best this country has to offer. And that man is John Kerry.

John Kerry understands the ideals of community, faith and service because they've defined his life. From his heroic service to Vietnam, to his years as a prosecutor and lieutenant governor, through two decades in the United States Senate, he's devoted himself to this country. Again and again, we've seen him make tough choices when easier ones were available.

His values and his record affirm what is best in us. John Kerry believes in an America where hard work is rewarded; so instead of offering tax breaks to companies shipping jobs overseas, he offers them to companies creating jobs here at home.

John Kerry believes in an America where all Americans can afford the same health coverage our politicians in Washington have for themselves.

John Kerry believes in energy independence, so we aren't held hostage to the profits of oil companies, or the sabotage of foreign oil fields.

John Kerry believes in the Constitutional freedoms that have made our country the envy of the world, and he will never sacrifice our basic liberties, nor use faith as a wedge to divide us.

And John Kerry believes that in a dangerous world war must be an option sometimes, but it should never be the first option.

You know, awhile back—awhile back I met a young man named Shamus in a V.F.W. Hall in East Moline, Illinois. He was a good-looking kid—six-two, six-three, clear eyed, with an easy smile. He told me he'd joined the Marines and was heading to Iraq the following week. And as I listened to him explain why he'd enlisted, the absolute faith he had in our country and its leaders, his devotion to duty and service, I thought this young man was all that any of us might ever hope for in a child.

But then I asked myself, "Are we serving Shamus as well as he is serving us?"

I thought of the 900 men and women—sons and daughters, husbands and wives, friends and neighbors, who won't be returning to their own hometowns. I thought of the families I've met who were struggling to get by without a loved one's full income, or whose loved ones had returned with a limb missing or nerves shattered, but still lacked long-term health benefits because they were Reservists.

When we send our young men and women into harm's way, we have a solemn obligation not to fudge the numbers or shade the truth about why they're going, to care for their families while they're gone, to tend to the soldiers upon their return, and to never ever go to war without enough troops to win the war, secure the peace and earn the respect of the world.

Now—Now let me be clear. Let me be clear. We have real enemies in the world. These enemies must be found. They must be pursued. And they must be defeated. John Kerry knows this. And just as Lieutenant Kerry did not hesitate to risk his life to protect the men who served with him in Vietnam, President Kerry will not hesitate one moment to use our military might to keep America safe and secure.

John Kerry believes in America. And he knows that it's not enough for just some of us to prosper—for alongside our famous individualism, there's another ingredient in the American saga, a belief that we're all connected as one people. If there is a child on the south side of Chicago who can't read, that matters to me, even if it's not my child. If there is a senior citizen somewhere who can't pay for their prescription drugs, and is having to choose between medicine and the rent, that makes my life poorer, even if it's not my grandparent. If there's an Arab American family being rounded up without benefit of an attorney or due process, that threatens my civil liberties.

It is that fundamental belief—It is that fundamental belief: I am my brother's keeper, I am my sister's keeper, that makes this country work. It's what allows us to pursue our individual dreams and yet still come together as one American family.

E pluribus unum: "Out of many, one."

Now even as we speak, there are those who are preparing to divide us—the spin masters, the negative ad peddlers who embrace the politics of "anything goes." Well, I say to them tonight, there is not a liberal America and a conservative America—there is the United States of America. There is not a Black America and a White America and Latino America and Asian America—there's the United States of America.

The pundits, the pundits like to slice-and-dice our country into Red States and Blue States; Red States for Republicans, Blue States for Democrats. But I've got news for them, too. We worship an "awesome God" in the Blue States, and we don't like federal agents poking around in our libraries in the Red States. We coach Little League in the Blue States and yes, we've got some gay friends in the Red States. There are patriots who opposed the war in Iraq and there are patriots who supported the war in Iraq. We are one people, all of us pledging allegiance to the stars and stripes, all of us defending the United States of America.

In the end—In the end—In the end, that's what this election is about. Do we participate in a politics of cynicism or do we participate in a politics of hope?

John Kerry calls on us to hope. John Edwards calls on us to hope.

I'm not talking about blind optimism here—the almost willful ignorance that thinks unemployment will go away if we just don't think about it, or the health care crisis will solve itself if we just ignore it. That's not what I'm talking about. I'm talking about something more substantial. It's the hope of slaves sitting around a fire singing freedom songs; the hope of immigrants setting out for distant shores; the hope of a young naval lieutenant bravely patrolling the Mekong Delta; the hope of a millworker's son who dares to defy the odds; the hope of a skinny kid with a funny name who believes that America has a place for him, too.

Hope—Hope in the face of difficulty. Hope in the face of uncertainty. The audacity of hope!

In the end, that is God's greatest gift to us, the bedrock of this nation. A belief in things not seen. A belief that there are better days ahead.

I believe that we can give our middle class relief and provide working families with a road to opportunity.

I believe we can provide jobs to the jobless, homes to the homeless, and reclaim young people in cities across America from violence and despair.

I believe that we have a righteous wind at our backs and that as we stand on the crossroads of history, we can make the right choices, and meet the challenges that face us.

America! Tonight, if you feel the same energy that I do, if you feel the same urgency that I do, if you feel the same passion that I do, if you feel the same hopefulness that I do—if we do what we must do, then I have no doubt that all across the country, from Florida to Oregon, from Washington to Maine, the people will rise up in November, and John Kerry will be sworn in as President, and John Edwards will be sworn in as Vice President, and this country will reclaim its promise, and out of this long political darkness a brighter day will come.

Thank you very much everybody. God bless you. Thank you. ○჻

Sources

Much of the information and many of the ideas in this work stem from a pair of fascinating, beautifully written books:

Obama, Barack. *Dreams from My Father: A Story of Race and Inheritance.* New York: Times Books, 1995; paperback edition, New York: Three Rivers Press, 2004.

Obama, Barack. *The Audacity of Hope: Thoughts on Reclaiming the American Dream.* New York: Crown Publishers, 2006; paperback edition: New York: Three Rivers Press, 2006.

CHAPTER 1
Stepping onto a World Stage

Charlton, Brian. "Obama's Sister Debuts as a Campaigner." *Associated Press,* May 12, 2007.

Obama, Barack. "A Life's Calling to Public Service." *Punahou Bulletin,* Fall 1999.

Pang, Gordon Y.K. "Democrats Call Obama Hawai'i's 'Third Senator.'" *Honolulu Advertiser,* December 17, 2004.

Ramler, Siegfried. Interview with the authors, 2008.

Vorsino, Mary. "Obama Pushes Message of Diversity." *Honolulu Star-Bulletin,* December 17, 2004.

CHAPTER 2
Starting School in Honolulu

Eldredge, Pal. Interviews with the authors, 2008.

Essoyan, Susan. "A Teacher's Hefty Influence." *Honolulu Star-Bulletin,* July 29, 2007.

Punahou: The History and Promise of a School of the Islands. Ed. Nelson Foster; Honolulu: Punahou School, 1992. See also: Punahou School Web site, www.Punahou.edu

135

CHAPTER 3
Hawai'i in the Time of Statehood

East-West Center.
See: www.eastwestcenter.org.

Guess Who's Coming to Dinner,
1987 film: Written by William Rose,
directed by Stanley Kramer.
Columbia Pictures.

J. Strom Thurmond in the Congressional Record, as recounted by
Gavan Daws: *Shoal of Time: A History of the Hawaiian Islands*, University of
Hawai'i Press, 1968.

"Loving Decision: 40 Years of
Legal Interracial Unions." National
Public Radio: *All Things Considered*,
June 11, 2007.

Obama, Barack, Sr. "Exit Interview
with John Griffin." *Honolulu Star-Bulletin*, June 1962.

Obama, Barack, Sr. "Interracial
Attitude Impresses." *Honolulu Star-Bulletin*, November, 1959.

Pilahi Paki description of Aloha: see
www.hawaii-nation.org/aloha.html.

South Pacific, Broadway musical, 1949:
Music by Richard Rodgers, lyrics
by Oscar Hammerstein II, book by
Oscar Hammerstein II and Joshua
Logan. Based upon *Tales of the South
Pacific*, by James A. Michener. Movie
version, 1958. Distributed by Magna
Corp. and Twentieth-Century Fox.

CHAPTER 4
A Woman from America, a Man from Africa.

"A Special Report: The Obama
Family Tree." *Chicago Sun-Times*,
September 9, 2007.

Chipman, Kim. "Obama Drive Gets
Inspiration from His White Mom
Born in Kansas." Bloomberg.com,
February 11, 2008.

Chipman, Kim and Wahyudi Soeri-aatmadja. "Obama's Jakarta Friends
Recall a Would-Be Leader." Bloomberg.com, February 25, 2008.

Cohen, Roger. "The Obamas
of the World." *New York Times*,
March 6, 2008.

Dobbs, Michael. "Obama Over-states Kennedy's Role in Helping
His Father." *Washington Post*,
March 30, 2008.

Griffin, John. Interview. *Honolulu
Advertiser*, November 28, 1959.

Griffin, John. Interview with Barack
Obama Sr. "Various Races Get Along
Better." *Honolulu Star-Bulletin*,
June 1962.

Jones, Tim. "Maya Soetoro-Ng:
Q&A." VIBE.com, August 27, 2007.

Martin, Jonathan. "Obama's Mother
Known Here as 'Uncommon.'" *Seattle
Times*, April 9, 2008.

Meaghar, Matt. "Barack Obama's Early Years in Indonesia." *Inside Edition*, May 6, 2008.

"Obama's Mom: Not Just a Girl from Kansas." *Chicago Tribune*, March 27, 2007.

Scott, Janny. "A Free-Spirited Wanderer Who Set Obama's Path." *New York Times*, March 14, 2008.

Sheridan, Michael. "Secrets of the Obama Family Unlocked." *Sunday Times* (London), January 28, 2007.

Thanawala, Sudhin. "Obama's Success Rooted in Hawai'i." *Associated Press*, February 14, 2008.

Wamari, Elly. "Obama Snr Went to U.S. on Scholarship but His Son Now Aims for White House." *The Nation, Nairobi*, June 5, 2008.

Williamson, Lucy. "Jakarta Classmates Recall Barry Obama." BBC News, April 19, 2008.

CHAPTER 5
Indonesia's Unity in Diversity

Bigalke, Terry. Interview with the authors, 2008.

Chipman, Kim and Wahyudi Soeriaatmadja. "Obama's Jakarta Friends Recall a Would-Be Leader." Bloomberg.com, December 31, 2007.

Cohen, Muhammad. "The Indonesian Candidate." *Asia Times*, February 19, 2008.

Cohen, Roger. "Obama's Indonesian Lessons." *The New York Times*, April 14, 2008.

Fornek, Scott. "A Special Report: The Obama Family Tree. Lolo Soetoro: "A piece of tiger meat." *Chicago Sun-Times*, September 9, 2007.

Meaghar, Matt. "Barack Obama's Early Years in Indonesia." *Inside Edition*, May 6, 2008.

Purdum, Todd. "Raising Obama: Politics and Power." *Vanity Fair*, March 2008.

Scharnberg, Kirsten and Kim Barker with Ray Gibson. "The Not-So-Simple Story of Barack Obama's Youth." *Chicago Tribune*, February 25, 2008.

Soetoro-Ng, Maya. Interview with the authors, 2008.

Williamson, Lucy. "Jakarta Classmates Recall Barry Obama." BBC News, April 19, 2008.

CHAPTER 6
Barry Meets His Father

"An Honest Government, A Hopeful Future," a speech by Barack Obama, University of Nairobi, August 28, 2006.

Eldredge, Pal. Interviews with the authors, 2008.

Nakaso, Dan. "Obama's Tutu a Hawai'i Banking Female Pioneer." *Honolulu Advertiser*, March 30, 2008.

CHAPTER 7
Choosing between Black and White

Agbayani, Amy. Interview with the authors, 2008.

Apo, Peter. "The Role Cultural Diversity Plays." See: www.peterapo.com; undated.

Ariyoshi, Rita. "Mean Old Mr. Sun Cho Lee and Ethnic Humor in Hawai'i." *Spirit of Aloha*, November-December 2004.

Eldredge, Pal. Interview with the authors, 2008.

"Obama Had Multiethnic Existence in Hawai'i." *Associated Press*, February 6, 2007.

Peterson, Tony. "What I Can Tell You About Barack Obama." *Honolulu Star-Bulletin*, February 15, 2008.

Purdum, Todd. "Raising Obama: Politics and Power." *Vanity Fair*, March 2008.

Scharnberg, Kirsten and Kim Barker with Ray Gibson. "The Not-So-Simple Story of Barack Obama's Youth." *Chicago Tribune*, February 25, 2008.

Solomon, Deborah. "All in the Family: Questions for Maya Soetoro-Ng." *New York Times, The Times Magazine*, January 20, 2008.

Steinhauser, Jennifer. "Charisma and a Search for Self in Obama's Hawai'i Childhood." *New York Times*, March 17, 2007.

Takaki, Ronald. Interview with the authors, 2008.

Tanji, Melissa. "Obama's Half-Sister Playing to Hawai'i Ties for Campaign." *Maui News*, February 17, 2008.

Walsh, Kenneth T. "Becoming Barack Obama." *U.S. News and World Report*, May 30, 2008.

CHAPTER 8
Hawai'i in the '70s

Abercrombie, Neil. Interview with the authors, 2008.

Eric Yamamoto. "The Significance of Local" in *Social Process in Hawai'i*, ed. Peter Manicas, McGraw Hill Inc, 1963.

Lueras, Leonard. "Hawai'i Super-Mixed by Interracial Marriage." *Honolulu Star-Bulletin* and *Honolulu Advertiser*, January 10, 1975.

Obama, Barack. "A Life's Calling to Public Service." *Punahou Bulletin*, Fall 1999.

"Punahou: The History and Promise of a School of the Islands." Edited by Nelson Foster; Honolulu: Punahou School, 1992. See also: Punahou School Web site, www.Punahou.edu.

Walsh, Kenneth T. "Becoming Barack Obama." *U.S. News and World Report*, May 30, 2008.

CHAPTER 9
Punahou School, Microcosm of Hawai'i

Heidel, Rev. John. Interview with the authors, 2008.

Husain, Laurel Bowers and Laurie Uemoto Chang. "Obama Encourages Students to Dream Big." *Punahou Bulletin*, Spring 2005.

Murphy, Austin. "Obama Discusses Hoops Memories at Punahou." *Sports Illustrated*, May 21, 2008.

Obama, Barack. "A Life's Calling to Public Service." *Punahou Bulletin*, Fall 1999.

"Punahou: The History and Promise of a School of the Islands." Ed. Nelson Foster; Honolulu: Punahou School, 1992.

CHAPTER 10
Barry O'Bomber

Brannon, Johnny. "Hawai'i's Imperfect Melting Pot A Big Influence on Young Obama." *Honolulu Advertiser*, February 10, 2007.

"For Obama, Sport Is Much More Than a Game." *Washington Post*, April 16, 2008.

Hoover, Will. "Obama's Declaration Still Thrills at Punahou." *Honolulu Advertiser*, February 11, 2007.

Murphy, Austin. "Obama Discusses Hoops Memories at Punahou." *Sports Illustrated*, May 21, 2008.

Reardon, Dave. "Coaching Teammates Eldredge, McLachlin Retire from Punahou." *Honolulu Star-Bulletin*, June 20, 2007.

Sanner, Ann. "Obama Says He Looked to Basketball in His Youth." *Associated Press*, April 15, 2008.

Silva, Mark. "How Much Game He Got?" *Chicago Tribune*, April 15, 2008.

Song, Jaymes. "Obama Finds Refuge, Identity in Basketball." *Associated Press*, June 16, 2008.

Tani, Carlyn. "A Kid Called Barry." *Punahou Bulletin*, Spring 2007.

Winfrey, Oprah. "Oprah's Cut with Barack Obama." *O, The Oprah Magazine*, November 2004.

CHAPTER 11
Turbulent Times in High School

Da Silva, Alexandre. "Isle Delegates and Associates Applaud Speech." *Honolulu Star-Bulletin*, July 28, 2004.

Haenisch, Richard. Interview with Johnny Brannon, *Honolulu Advertiser.*

Kovaleski, Serge F. "Old Friends Say Drugs Played Bit Part in Obama's Young Life." *New York Times*, February 9, 2008.

Murphy, Austin. "Obama Discusses Hoops Memories at Punahou." *Sports Illustrated*, May 21, 2008.

Nichols, Hans. "Media Surfs Obama's Past." ThePolitico.com, March 14. 2007.

Reyes, B.J. "Punahou Left Lasting Impression on Obama." *Honolulu Star-Bulletin*, February 8, 2007.

Serrano, Richard A. "Obama's Peers Didn't See His Angst." *Los Angeles Times*, March 11, 2007.

Shikina, Robert. "Hawai'i Gatherings Nurture Support for Obama." *Honolulu Star-Bulletin*, April 1, 2007.

Steinhauser, Jennifer. "Charisma and A Search for Self in Obama's Hawai'i Childhood." *The New York Times*, March 17, 2007.

Thanawala, Sudhin. "Barry Learned to Like Punahou." *Associated Press*, March 30, 2008.

"When Barry Became Barack." *Newsweek*, March 31, 2008.

CHAPTER 12
Hawai'i's Multicultural Milieu

Davis, Frank Marshall. "This is Paradise." *Black Moods: Collected Poems*, University of Illinois Press, 2002.

Takara, Kathryn Waddell. "Blacks in Hawai'i had a certain fluidity." *Frank Marshall Davis: Black Labor Activist and Outsider Journalist: Social Movements in Hawai'i.* See: www2.Hawaii.edu/~takara/frank_marshall_davis.htm.

Takara, Kathryn Waddell. Interview with the authors, 2008.

CHAPTER 13
The Lessons of Hawai'i

DePledge, Derrick. "Punahou Gets Inouye Apology for Obama Barb." *Honolulu Advertiser*, February 26, 2008.

"Letters to the Editor." *Honolulu Star-Bulletin* and *Honolulu Advertiser*, February 2008.

"Picture of O'ahu Site Keeps Obama Grounded." *Associated Press*, May 18, 2007.

CHAPTER 14
The Campaign in Hawai'i

Borreca, Richard. "Obama Touts Isle Ties in Campaign Call." *Honolulu Star-Bulletin*, February 16, 2008.

DePledge, Derrick. "Campaigns Send in Family." *Honolulu Advertiser*, February 16, 2008.

Hillyer, Beth. "Obama Campaign Down to the Wire." KHNL-TV, February 18, 2008.

Loe, Stacy. "Interview with Obama via Satellite." KGMB-TV, February 16, 2008.

Malveaux, Suzanne. "Reporting from Hawai'i." CNN, CNN.com, February 19, 2008.

"Obama Caller Gets Surprise— Candidate's Grandmother." KITV, February 15, 2008.

Park, Gene. "Obama's Half-Sister Helps Kick Off Local Campaign." *Honolulu Star-Bulletin*, May 13, 2007.

Perry and Price, radio show, KSSK, Honolulu Hawai'i, December 2007.

Yamane, Marisa. "Barack Obama Satellite Interview." KHON-TV, February 17, 2008.

Further reading:

Coffman, Tom. *The Island Edge of America: A Political History of Hawai'i.* University of Hawai'i Press, 2003.

Daws, Gavan. *Shoal of Time: A History of the Hawaiian Islands.* University of Hawai'i Press, 1968.

Fuchs, Lawrence H. *Hawaii Pono: A Social History of Hawai'i.* New York: Harcourt, Brace and World, 1961.

Mendell, David. *Obama: From Promise to Power.* HarperCollinsBooks, 2007.

Michener, James A. *Hawaii.* New York: Bantam Books, 1960.

Takaki, Ronald. *A Different Mirror: A History of Multicultural America.* New York: Back Bay Books, 1994.

INDEX

ACKNOWLEDGMENTS

The authors wish to thank everyone who offered ideas and inspiration in their interviews. Special thanks go to those who lent a hand in helping prepare this work for book, including Michael H. Anderson, Frederika Bain, Bernice Bowers, Beverly Creamer, George Engebretson, Janice Nuckols, Marisa Oshiro, Maya Soetoro-Ng, John Strobel, Kathryn Waddel Takara and the many friends and teachers who knew Barack Obama at Punahou School.

About the Authors

During his career as a journalist with *The Honolulu Advertiser* and *Honolulu Star-Bulletin*, Stu Glauberman covered many beats including education, politics, business and Hawaiian affairs. He has traveled widely and also reported from Asia.

Jerry Burris is Hawai'i's foremost political analyst, having reported and commented on politics for readers of *The Honolulu Advertiser* and Honolulu television viewers for more than 30 years.